New Hampshire—A Visual History
Seacoast

First NH Banks is proud to have a part in preserving the recorded history of the Seacoast through presentation of this pictorial account of the area's development and progress.

This volume is part of a series produced to preserve the rich heritage of the Granite State. In that regard, we wish to acknowledge and express our sincere appreciation to the authors, the University of New Hampshire, and New Hampshire Public Television for their creative contributions.

Each page of the Seacoast is a salute to the men and women whose untiring efforts created a region rich in cultural, educational, commercial, industrial, and charitable enterprises of which all can be justly proud.

First NH Banks is very much a part of New Hampshire's legacy, and we dedicate this book to all of our citizens—past, present, and future.

①First NH Banks

This book is dedicated to four grandmothers

Cora Chatterton MacGregor

Bertha Channell Gilmore

Mary Cherry Blackwood

Lillian May Ingmire

the SeaCoast

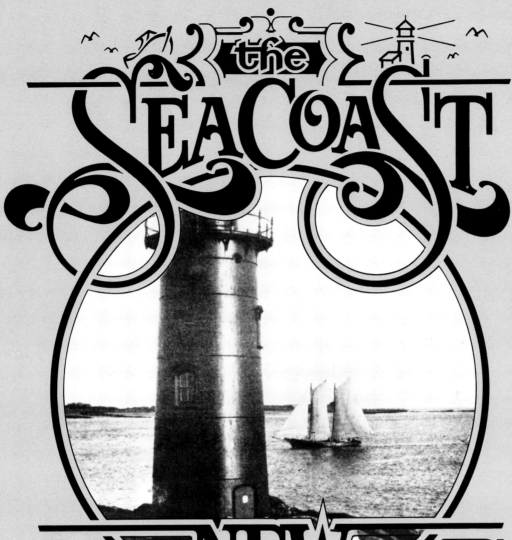

NEW HAMPSHIRE

A VISUAL HISTORY

Robert Gilmore & Bruce Ingmire

THE
DONNING COMPANY
PUBLISHERS
NORFOLK / VIRGINIA BEACH

The Donning Company/Publishers
5659 Virginia Beach Boulevard
Norfolk, Virginia 23502

Edited by Liliane McCarthy
Richard A. Horwege, Senior Editor

Library of Congress Cataloging-in-Publication Data:

Gimore, Robert C., 1922-
  The seacoast, New Hampshire.

  Bibliography: p.
  Includes index.
  1. Atlantic Coast (N.H.)—History, Local—Pictorial works.
2. Coasts—New Hampshire—History—Pictorial works. 3. New Hampshire—History, Local—Pictorial works. I. Ingmire, Bruce E. II. Title.
F35.G49   1989   974.2'00946   88-36265
ISBN 0-89865-736-9

Printed in the United States of America

CONTENTS

INTRODUCTION

It would truly be exciting if pictures of the original New Hampshire settlements could be miraculously produced, but this is of course a fantasy. We have summarized the history of this state from English colonization to the present. Photographs are available for only the last hundred years. In many cases the photos depict the same site or neighborhood in several different eras. We have been given pictures from a number of private collections so that we can demonstrate that families have flourished and contributed to the seacoast history over these years. We would like to thank the Berry family, Mr. and Mrs. William Warren, Richard Candee, Robert Whitehouse, Mr. and Mrs. George Frost Sawyer, Dorothy Watson, Barbara Myers, Jane Porter, Mrs. Louis DeRochemont and her daughter Virginia DeRochemont, Rebecca Marden, Mrs. William Cotter, Mr. and Mrs. James Barker Smith, Mrs. Dorothy Henderson, Mrs. Dorothy Gilman, Jeanne Mitchell, Carol Rindfleisch, Pro Portsmouth, the Athenaeum, and the historical societies of Newington, Rye, Newmarket, and Exeter.

1
OUT
OF
MASSACHUSETTS

The brief, eighteen-mile stretch of coastline claimed by modern New Hampshire can be observed off-shore from the Isles of Shoals with scarcely a turn of the head, for it is bracketed between the sweep of Cape Anne to the south and the low rise of Mount Agamenticus on the north. In the seafaring days, when Mount Agamenticus appeared to the sailors as the Three Turks Heads, the great inland bay that forms the heart of the seacoast was unseen. Yet that Great Bay served as the source of food for the huge schools of fish that lured these European fishermen. As the voyagers approached the river's mouth, the Piscataqua acquired definition and gradually the broad estuary opened into the inland bay. Washed by the tides and fed by a multitude of tributaries that wound through the countryside, the bay served as a sparkling focus for the region. Here beside the waterfalls and on the shores of the Great Bay, the first European settlements appeared long ago.

In the twilight of the Elizabethan Age, ships bearing English adventurers began to frequent that part of the coast that came to be New Hampshire. Martin Pring, an intrepid young seaman, sailed into the Piscataqua estuary in 1603 and became the first Englishman to leave an account of his visit including a favorable impression of the harbor. Eleven years later the hero of Jamestown, the legendary Capt. John Smith cruised the Isles of Shoals,

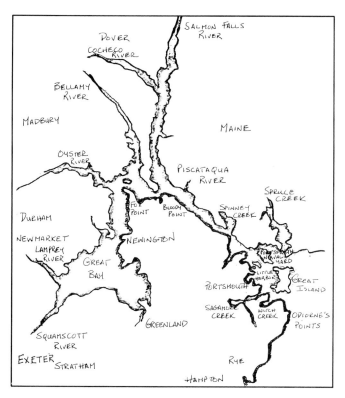

modestly naming them the Smith Isles. Smith, a brilliant propagandist and acute observer, gifted in self-dramatization, drew an enthusiastic picture in his *Description of New England* and alerted his fellow-countrymen to the possibilities of colonial development. Among those whose interest he sparked was Sir Fernando Gorges. Gorges had become embroiled in the politics surrounding Queen Elizabeth and the earl of Essex. Bored with court intrigue, he repaired to his beloved West Country, where the tales of fishermen provoked his curiosity about the New World and culminated in the organization of the Council for New England over which he presided and whose policies he shaped. A joint-stock company, the council received jurisdiction by a grant of James I over the territory from the fortieth to the forty-eighth parallels.

Among the other members of the council was John Mason of Portsmouth in Hampshire, southeastern England. Mason was perceived as an ally of Gorges. From Plymouth, a center for much enthusiasm for the New World, hailed David Thompson who became the first

settler in New Hampshire. Thompson was supported by three investors from Plymouth. In 1619 he purchased an island in Shawmut Harbor, later Boston, to which he apparently made a trip but did not take up residence. He returned to New England in the spring of 1623 with his family. At that time he erected a trading post on Little Harbor on the Piscataqua. Miles Standish visited him that summer, and Thompson left for Plymouth with Standish. There is no record of his returning permanently to the Piscataqua, where his home became a meetingplace for sojourners who called it Rendezvous. Records from Boston Harbor report Thompson's presence there. He died in 1626 on Thompson Island.

In the interim Sir Fernando Gorges, who was identified with the royalist cause in the burgeoning English Civil War, found his attention continually diverted from his interests in the New World. He never visited America but dispatched his son Robert to New England as a governor general in the same year that Thompson left. Among the members of Capt. Robert Gorges' band of settlers who

The drowned forest off Boar's Head, Rye, New Hampshire, near the old cable house. Some ten thousand years ago the forest flourished and eventually petri- *fied. It has been visible only twice in the last century, in 1898 and again in 1958, when this photograph was taken. Both occasions followed a major storm.* *Courtesy of the Rye Historical Society and Rebecca B. Marden*

arrived at Wessagusset, site of the future Weymouth, Massachusetts, was Thomas Walford, who moved north to Shawmut Harbor, where he met David Thompson. The younger Gorges encountered financial difficulties and returned to England. Sir Fernando abandoned his efforts in Massachusetts and concentrated on settlements in Maine, where he supported settlers at Gorgeana, modern-day York.

In 1629 John Mason in concert with Gorges began to organize colonizers for settlement upon the Piscataqua. Mason's efforts would prove long-lasting although not lucrative for him personally. It is important to note that 1629 marked the beginning of the eleven-year period of personal rule by King Charles I, a time of escalating confrontation between king and Parliament, culminating in the battles of the Civil War. Eventually Gorges and Mason divided these northern settlements between themselves. Shortly thereafter, in 1635, Mason died, before King Charles I had a chance to confirm the arrangement.

In those years when the infant colony that Mason called Hampshire struggled to gain a precarious foothold on the Atlantic coast, the English homeland found its attention monopolized by the struggle between Parliament and king. During this time and just days after Mason and Gorges had received their grant on the Piscataqua, a London fishmonger, Edward Hilton, was also granted rights to land in the same vicinity. It is possible the council assumed that Mason was intending to lumber, farm, trap, and herd livestock and that Hilton would engage in fishing. Hilton and his compatriots settled on Dover Point. Lord Saye and Sele, a Puritan, purchased from one Edward Hilton his rights to land on the tributaries of the Piscataqua. Hilton moved just to the south on land that eventually became part of Exeter, New Hampshire.

As a result of the sale of Hilton's Patent, a band of Puritans moved northward from Salem in 1631. Led by Capt. Thomas Wiggin and Richard Waldron, the Puritans settled on Dover Point at the mouth of Great Bay. That same year a number of factors under the direction of Captain Walter Neal arrived at Little Harbor. They appar-

This photo shows the tree lined Piscataqua River in the late nineteenth century. Earlier, the forest contained pines near the shoreline that were 200 feet tall.
Courtesy of the Athenaeum

Another view of the Piscataqua. By the early 1800s the entire virgin forest had been stripped, and most of the soil had been depleted of its nutrients. Notice the settlements along the shoreline.
Courtesy of the Athenaeum

ently occupied the abandoned Rendezvous. Tradition and early attempts to locate this site have operated on the assumption that Odiorne's Point, named for a later owner, was the location of the so-called Great House. Recently, however, intensive study of the early documents has led some to conclude that there is much evidence indicating that Sanders Point is the site of Rendezvous. John Sanders was another of the men who came in Capt. Robert Gorges' band of colonizers. Whether he lived at the site was never indicated in the records. Nevertheless, both Neal and his successor, Ambrose Gibbons, left records of their occupancy of Rendezvous. Gibbon's son-in-law was in possession of the land by 1645.

Despite the confusion of claims, Mason plunged ahead with his schemes. With Gorges he formed the Laconia Company in the pursuit of a fortune in raw materials. Capt. Walter Neal became the on-site agent of the Laconia Company at the Piscataqua. Precisely how many men arrived in 1631 is a matter of speculation. Many names associated with those of the original party have turned up in records of earlier settlements. A notable example is the previously mentioned Thomas Walford, who had been in New England for nearly ten years. By virtue of Walford's earlier association with the Gorges family and his familiarity with the Piscataqua, he became a resident after being banished in 1631 from Charlestown, Massachusetts, as a non-conformist.

Neal settled two sections of the Piscataqua, Little

The University of New Hampshire conducted an archaeological dig at the site of the Seabrook Nuclear Station. Native Americans inhabited the site from 1800 B. C. until just before the arrival of the English. The white flecks represent the remains of shellfish that the nomadic Algonkian Indians ate during their annual visit to the site.
Courtesy of Professor Charles Bolian and the University of New Hampshire Media Services

This artifact, found in the excavations at Seabrook, is from the late Woodland period (about A. D. 1000 to A. D. 1600). It was used to make holes in the hides, which would then be sewn together. University of New Hampshire Professor Charles Bolian was in charge of the work.
Courtesy of Professor Charles Bolian and the University of New Hampshire Media Services

Harbor and Newichannock (Salmon Falls), but did not succeed in developing a profitable enterprise for Mason. Within five years of its inception, the Laconia Company ceased to exist. Nevertheless after Neal's departure, the remaining settlers and interlopers had developed enough commerce and mutual support to provide for a year-round existence. One of Neal's last contributions to the settlements at the Piscataqua was to meet with the Puritan leader Thomas Wiggin and arrange for a mutually agreeable division of the Piscataqua and its resources.

The meeting at a point of land in the river was a peaceful arrangement whereby the lands at the mouth of the Piscataqua were to be controlled by royalist forces directed by Neal and under the auspices of Mason. Wig-

gin's Puritan followers were to remain inland on Dover Point and the point upon which the meeting had been held. That point of the peninsula came to be called Bloody Point in an ironic reference to the peaceful meeting. Each rival chose part of a powerful falls in a more northern region of the Piscataqua for power to operate mills. Neal's compatriot Gibbons took command at Newichannock and Wiggin's compatriot Richard Waldron took over at Cocheco Falls. The amicable arrangement lasted until the early 1650s.

Eventually Gibbons replaced Neal, and Thomas Warnerton replaced Gibbons, who abandoned the Lower Piscataqua for Durham Point. Slowly some other Puritans from Massachusetts migrated north, either because they

*Depiction of a witch by Ivy of today's
Witches' Brew on Market Street. The
earliest settlers to New Hampshire
included the Walford familly, who lived
among the Indians in Shawmut (later
Boston) Harbor in the 1620s before they
trekked north. Many of the early colonial women learned about the medi-
cinal herbs of the North Amiercan
continent from the Indian medicine
men. Jane Walford's apparent association with the Indian doctors earned
her a reputation as a witch. Indian
medicine men earned their titles of
witch doctors from association with
women like Jane, who were community
healers and midwives.
Photo by Bruce E. Ingmire*

*The second Thomas Walford Plantation
and now the the farm of John Hett, who
intends to leave the land in trust.
From the collection of Bruce E. Ingmire*

were banished or in search of land. In 1635, when a hurricane smashed into New England, it wrecked the *Angel Gabriel*, a small wooden vessel, at Pemiquid, Maine. Four survivors, William Furber, Samuel Haines, Richard Tuttle, and Robert Burnham soon arrived in the Piscataqua. Like Samuel Haines, who became the longest serving deacon of the First Church of Christ in Portsmouth, they remained strong advocates of Puritanism.

The legacy of the early claims was to hover over New Hampshire citizens for nearly a century. At the time it often contributed to a divisive political climate, as certain settlers leaned toward leading contenders for the original rights. When there were legal challenges to land titles, other disputes flourished, accusations of witchcraft appeared, and people became generally unsettled. However, from the perspective of hindsight it appears that in the long run, the battles about the title to land drew most of the settlers together. Puritan and royalist, landowner and tenant, Province leader and minister were forced to band together in opposition to royal decrees giving new royal favorites claim to New Hampshire's land. Many early forms of resistance to excesses of royal power under Charles II laid the groundwork for the growth of an independent spirit and a sense of wellbeing and power that came to be identified as Yankee. Eventually these men would turn against George III.

But not just individual stragglers from Massachusetts arrived in New Hampshire. John Wheelwright from East Anglia and a number of his relatives and friends who had been supporters of Anne Hutchinson, arrived on the

This is the seventeenth-century Dame Garrison from Dover, New Hampshire, now on Central Avenue in Dover and part of the Woodman Institute. This is the only extant New Hampshire garrison still in its original state. Garrison *is the term that was applied to homes constructed to double as military posts in the event of attacks.*
Courtesy of Robert C. Whitehouse

Squamscott River a few miles to the west of the Atlantic coast and founded the town of Exeter. Hutchinson, a kinswoman of Winthrop and related by marriage to Wheelwright, had challenged the authority of Winthrop and the authority of the written word by leading religious discussions and meetings in the Bay Colony. In what became known as the Antinomian Controversy, she and her followers asserted that the laity, with God's Grace, could interpret holy writ as authentically as ordained clergy. "She knew much," wrote Charles Francis Adams, "but she talked out of proportion to her knowledge." Brought before magistrates, she was banished. Wheelwright's departure from Massachusetts and subsequent arrival in New Hampshire resulted from this upheaval.

Indeed some rather amazing characters emerged from the alleged somber and sober Puritan masses of the Bay Colony. One of the most colorful Puritans was the minister Stephen Batchelder. At age seventy he crossed the Atlantic. Eventually he was called to fill the pulpit at Lynn, just north of Boston. He had been a member of churches in England that ascribed to a Familist persuasion, a radical religious philosophy. He had joined a group called the Plough Society, and his arrival in New England coincided with the millennial spirit so common among the participants in the English migration.

In Lynn, Batchelder was accused of gathering a church without sufficient permission. The Lynn congregation was thrown into an uproar. Some of the congregation insisted Batchelder must be dismissed while others supported him. Batchelder led his supporters to a region of northern Massachusetts called Winnecunnet,

which they named Hampton. A few interlopers had already established themselves at the location, but the new arrivals and the old planters soon ironed out their differences. Here shortly thereafter Batchelder came into contention with his assistant, Timothy Dalton. Dalton was a hard-line Puritan and challenged the minister more for his behavior than for religious beliefs. Eventually charges of infidelity surfaced. Batchelder denied the charges, but in the introspective and torturous self examination so common among Puritans, he stepped forward the next week and admitted that he had contemplated adultery.

Eventually Batchelder left Hampton for Portsmouth and married Mary Beadle, who became pregnant when the minister was in his eighties. The town wags were quick to point out that the likely father was one Rogers, and court depositions, admonitions, and fines substantiated the fact. The redoubtable minister returned to England, and in his nineties took his fourth wife. His later escapades have allowed historians to assume the earlier allegations were true even though no victim was ever produced.

Settlement of the future New Hampshire proceeded. Gentlemen in royal offices in England scrutinized inadequate maps, defined grants, and produced descriptions that caused grief to settlers on the other side of the ocean. With sketchy geographical knowledge, the leaders of the Massachusetts Bay Colony insisted that they had legitimate right to Hampton and Exeter, if not the whole Piscataqua. Wiggin and Waldron and the Puritan settlers concurred with this reasoning. In the early 1640s certain citizens signed submissions to the Bay Colony in

14

This garrison of the Smith family was located on Lubberland Road near Great Bay between Durham and Newmarket. David Dan built this garrison in 1695 but was killed by Indians the following year while trying to reach the safety of the fortification. At that time Capt. John Smith purchased the property, and it remained in the Smith family until 1825, when the captain's great-granddaughter, Peggy, died. It was a typical garrison with a second story overhang. It was demolished in 1880.
Courtesy of
Mr. and Mrs. George Frost Sawyer

hopes of future favor. Richard Waldron even served in the Massachusetts General Court, rising to the position of Speaker. Often characterized as perpetrators of a land grab, these Puritans in fact were supported by a large contingent of the settlers who favored the authority and organization of Puritan Massachusetts while they eschewed its excesses.

Many settlers had been propelled north by Anglican and royalist sympathies. Men like Henry Sherburne would carry on a vigorous opposition to the Puritan ministry and leadership. During the 1640s, however, things remained at a standstill, especially in the Lower Piscataqua or Strawbery Banke as some people with a certain originality had come to call the settlement located at the mouth of the river, primarily on an island called Great Island and a neck of land called Portsmouth Neck.

The Piscataqua had representation in the Massachusetts General Court, and the settlers were given a certain measure of autonomy in voting. They also had some choice in magistrates. The courts met on a regular basis. In 1648 the codified Laws and Liberties of Massachusetts were compiled, and in the following year printed copies became available. Puritanism had gained impetus from the victories at Naseby and Marston Moor, and ships arriving in the spring of 1649 brought news of the death of the English king at the hands of Parliament. In short order tensions in the community were reflected in numerous accusations.

Witchcraft was a subject of three court appearances in the summer session. John Crowder arrived home after a substantial absence to learn that his wife was heavy with child. Within days charges were pressed and his wife's

servant, Anne Wormwood, testified that Henry Taylor had been the culprit. By the summer's end Anne had delivered a baby boy, and both she and her lover were hanged from respective gallows in Boston where all capital punishments were carried out. Puritan justice was the swift justice of the Old Testament. Many years later a batchelor named John Crowther died in Kittery. He may have been the rejected son of the cuckolded captain.

By the mid-seventeenth century, the settlement at Strawbery Banke was comprised of approximately fifty families and contained about five hundred men and women. In 1652 the towns of Portsmouth, Massachusetts, and Kittery, Maine, were carved out of sections of Dover. Directed by Capt. Brian Pendleton of the Massachusetts General Court, the newly created Portsmouth made grants to forty-five male heads of families, and most of the grants amounted to restatements of existing holdings. One of the largest blocks of land fell to Thomas Walford, his son Jeremiah, and his four sons-in-law. All of the land that was allotted was already occupied by the owners on Great Island and Sanders Neck except for several large tracts which were owned by the Cutts brothers to the north at a place called Cutts Cove. Unlike the original settlers, Pendleton insisted upon the creation of a town common on Great Island.

Immediately the town began a search for a settled minister. Samuel Dudley of Exeter was called and served the town whose population increased with new arrivals from Massachusetts. Eventually they chose a twenty-five-year-old Harvard graduate and Ipswich native, Joshua Moodey. For the next forty years Moodey would have

Madame Ursula Cutts, the young second wife and widow of Pres. John Cutts, built this mansion, once located on present-day Woodbury Avenue, after his death in 1681. Her son-in-law was Richard Waldron, Jr., and five years after Richard Waldron, Sr., was killed by Indians in a reprisal, Madame Ursula was killed by Indians in an early July 1694 raid heralding the beginning of King William's War.
Courtesy of the Athenaeum

an influence on Portsmouth that would never again be equaled.

PURITANS

In 1647 royalist Sir Francis Gorges, who had personally directed much of the northern settlements, died. In 1650 Joseph Mason, a royalist in retreat, initiated a suit in Old Norfolk County Court. At the time Joseph Mason represented the interests of the family of John Mason, who had invested in the colony on the Piscataqua in the 1630s. Upon John Mason's death his widow, Ann, had instructed her husband's factors "to shift for themselves." As a result of this suit, Puritan leaders in the Bay Colony initiated an effort to tighten their control on two disputed areas, Piscataqua and Martha's Vineyard. Bay Colony leaders dispatched Thomas Mayhew to the Vineyard and Capt. Brian Pendleton to the Piscataqua.

Bay Colonists had been coming north from Massachusetts for years. By 1651 the conviction of Mary Beadle Batcheldor (Batchillor) to submit to branding of a letter on her face for adultery with George Rogers gives a clear indication that the stricter Puritan morality was showing its

face in the Piscataqua. Pendleton arrived with three sons and soon purchased land on Great Island. He was able to encourage the citizens of the old royalist enclave to organize a new town and confirm its status in the form of records and petitions to the General Court.

As a result, the townsmen at Great Island, Sandy Beach, and Strawbery Banke elected a leadership that reflected the large land owners. In 1652 the new name, Portsmouth, was confirmed by the General Court. The eastern shore of the river system was also organized by Pendleton into a separate political entity called Kittery. In the same year the new leaders confirmed the basic land arrangements of the freemen. The compact arrangement of enclosed fields was retained. Although Pendleton and some of the others came from areas which had open field systems, it appears that the time-consuming experience of this farming method in communities that they had inhabited led them to prefer the enclosed field system. Furthermore, it appears that the Piscataqua had become, like Ipswich, predominantly reliant upon husbandry. The next serious consideration was the assignment of salt marsh for the salt hay that it contained.

A photo of Sarah H. Foster's watercolor of the Capt. Thomas Thompson House, located next to the Langdon House museum on Pleasant Street. Thompson, the commander of the Raleigh, *built the house about 1780. At that time it was a waterfront home looking over the mill pond. The house remains a private home, and a recent asking price was three-quarters of a million dollars. Courtesy of the Athenaeum*

The other towns—Dover, Exeter, and Hampton—continued their allegiance to Massachusetts. These towns developed an agricultural base as well as a dependence upon lumber for their "cash crop." Dover had been reduced to about a third of its previous size but still contained a part of present-day Portsmouth-Bloody Point. The town records of Portsmouth contain various entries about the study and confirmation of the respective boundaries of these towns and the beginnings of highway construction. These towns continued to depend upon the pursuits of agriculture and husbandry, but Portsmouth under the leadership of the acquisitive Puritan leaders soon became the commercial leader.

By 1660 a second Portsmouth land division corrected any discrepancies created by the first division. This second division also dispersed more of the common lands, underlining the commitment to enclosed fields and self-sufficiency. In this second division sons who attained the ags of twenty-one and daughters of eighteen received land as well. This dispersal of land to women is a significant item. In some cases land was distributed to widows in other areas. The decision to treat women in an equal measure according to their social status was an important New England innovation.

More importantly for the emergence of the New Hampshire seacoast was the decision to settle a minister at Portsmouth. Dover had developed a pattern of itinerancy: Leverich, Burdette, Larkin, Maude, and Samuel Dudley served the citizens. The arrival of Joshua Moodey, Harvard trained and Bay Colony bred, marked the arrival of the Christ Church of Massachusetts in New Hampshire. Soon Dover settled John Pike, who had been raised in the Ipswich-Newbury area, as had Joshua Moodey. Pike married Moodey's daughter. Moodey's Harvard mate, Seaborn Cotton, was soon settled at Hampton. As Congregationalism emerged in New England these men joined forces with Exeter's Samuel Dudley, son of another prominent Boston family, and created a Puritan network closely aligned with the Boston clerical leadership.

The religious values soon meshed with the commercial ethic to bring more Boston investments into the region. Soon William Paine of the north shore and Thomas Broughton, Thomas Lake, and Valentine Hill of Boston were wielding vast commercial influence. Joining

17

with the Cutts, who had married into the Starr, Fernside, and Hull families, this network formed an oligarchy of potent influence. The Waldron and Wiggin families, who had controlled some of the timber up the Salmon River, were soon drawn into the oligarchy by the election of Richard Waldron as Speaker of the Bay Colony General Court. A neutral figure unaligned to any town around Boston, Waldron not only represented the inclusion of the Piscataqua into the fold of Massachusetts but provided authority to its leadership.

While the Piscataqua had experienced the tight family bonds of the era, with the arrival of the Bay Colonists, the Puritan order became firm. Moodey, who was in communication with leaders like Increase Mather, nonetheless drew his ministry from the lessons of ministers like Shepard of Rowley and Parker, who had led his parents into New England. There was an understanding of inspiration. The Piscataqua drew Quakers and Baptists, and many settled in Kittery. Moodey spent less time drawing lines to keep people out and more effort in drawing them in.

Yet with the Restoration in 1660 the old royalist sympathizers like Henry Sherburne agitated for an Anglican church. With the arrival in 1664-1665 of the Nichols Commission sent by the king to begin to reestablish royal authority, tensions mounted in the Piscataqua. Puritans like Stileman, Pendleton, Partridge and others had arrived from the Bay Colony. As a result, deeply religious men were forced to abandon New Hampshire. John

Photo of the Pennhallow House at Strawbery Banke, Inc. in 1988 and a house (far right) that was moved to the location about the time of the Civil War. It had been the home of Samuel Pennhallow, Speaker of the General Assembly, in 1699, Treasurer of the Province, and the author of The History of the Wars of New England with the Eastern Indians, *published in Boston by Samuel Gerrish and Daniel Henchmen in 1726.*
Photo by Bruce E. Ingmire

Martin, Benjamin Hull, John Onion, and Henry Dunn joined others from the North Shore and headed to New Jersey to seek religious freedom. Others, led by Anthony Emery, fled to Rhode Island. The towns of Piscataway, New Jersey, and Portsmouth, Rhode Island, owe their settlement to men who fled the Piscataqua for reasons of conscience.

Until 1679 the colony prospered. Indian wars caused some consternation in 1675, and soon the king separated the New Hampshire region from Massachusetts. This set off a flurry of political difficulties. John Cut and the Puritans were named to leadership positions, but soon the king drew the net tighter by sending a governor who conducted his office with outrageous contempt for the

"provincials." Moodey was driven from the colony. He was quickly invited to a high position at the First Church in Boston, and because of his ability to draw people to his ministry soon came in conflict with the Mathers over the witchcraft hysteria in Salem. Moodey personally helped a jailed witch and her husband escape to New York, where they were protected by Governor Fletcher.

In 1693 Moodey returned to Portsmouth and died in 1697. Pike remained in Dover. By then the Glorious Revolution had resolved the problematic succession and New England settled back down to business. The growth of the British empire had signaled new and important commercial outlets for the oligarchy now firmly in control of business in New Hampshire.

2
FROM COLONIAL RELIGION TO PROVINCIAL COMMERCE

In the 1880s, Charles Bell in his *History of the Town of Exeter* vividly described the intricate waterways of sea-coast New Hampshire. "The River Piscataqua," he wrote, "which forms the boundary next the sea between New Hampshire and Maine, may, with its tributaries, be rudely represented by a man's left hand and wrist laid upon a table, back upwards and fingers wide apart. The thumb would stand for the Salmon Falls or Newichannock River, the third for Lamprey River and the fourth for Exeter or Squamscot River; while the palm of the hand represent the Great Bay, into which most of those streams pour their waters, and the wrist the Piscataqua proper."

*Contemporary recreation of eighteenth-
century lumbering by University of New
Hampshire students and staff.
Courtesy of the University
of New Hampshire.*

*Another photograph of the same
reenactment.
Courtesy of the University of New
Hampshire Media Services;
photo by Ronald Bergeron*

Another photograph of the same reenactment.
Courtesy of the University of New Hampshire Media Services; photo by Ronald Bergeron

As the compact Puritan settlement gave way, the settlers turned to the hinterlands for their livelihood. The Piscataqua proved an efficient thoroughfare by which to reach the natural resources—furs and lumber. The vast salt marshes and adjacent plains soon became home to large herds of cows and sheep, and a familiar lifestyle developed for the English settlers who had come from Suffolk, Wiltshire, Essex, and Hampshire. The sea invited an eastward perspective, and thus the coastal farmers, drawing forest resources from the Piscataqua hinterland, established themselves as merchants by developing a commercial network with Europe, the Caribbean, and ports to the south. The abundance of fish and the virgin growth of oak and pine spreading to the rivers' banks provided that wedding of forest and sea that determined the course of the region's economic development.

Early in the seventeenth century, the settlers began to build ships in Dover, from which Portsmouth and Kittery were separated in 1652. By the end of the century, ships ranging in size from the flat-bottomed gundalows to the formidable warship *Falkland,* constructed at Portsmouth for the Royal Navy shortly after 1688, were launched.

A rising Puritan oligarchy was led by men who gained their fortunes as shipwrights. Their families—Cutts, Hunkings, Hulls, Vaughans, Millets, Bickfords, and Meserves—remained active in shipbuilding for generations. English shipwrights who had come to these shores were soon succeeded by American-born craftsmen. William Saltonstall has described in his work *Ports of the Piscataqua* the many small sloops constructed on creeks below the fall line or even, on occasion, in the woods.

These ships took shape in the winter, and great teams of oxen laboriously hauled them through the snow to the nearest river, where they floated downstream with the melting of the ice.

Ships built and maintained from the resources of the forests carried fish and lumber to southern Europe and the West Indies. In the Indies they boarded the rum, molasses, sugar, vanilla, and salt which they then transported to the Carolinas, Virginia, and Maryland, where some of the returning cargo was exchanged for rice, flour, pork, and tar. The combined cargo was transported back to Portsmouth markets. Occasionally goods came directly to the Piscataqua, bypassing the south. In some cases aggressive captains also transported slaves. Several blacks had become residents of the Piscataqua by the turn of the eighteenth century. One, known as Black Will, spent much time in the courts, where young women accused him of what might be termed "an alienation of affections." By the mid-eighteenth century few upper-class homes existed without household slaves.

The catalogue of colonial wars each bore the name of the contemporaneous British sovereign. The list of names—King William, Queen Anne, and King George—also reflects the number of changes on the English throne at the end of the Stuart period and the beginning of the Hanoverian dynasty, as well as general European political turmoil. The military activity merged with the commercial activity in the Piscataqua. From King William's War in 1689 to the end of King George's War in 1748, the flow of shipping from the Piscataqua met obstacles from French and Spanish vessels and privateers and, through trading

*Ship construction at Shattuck's Shipyard
in Newington during World War I. Ships
were built in much the same manner
during the seventeenth and eighteenth
centuries.*
*Courtesy of the University of New
Hampshire Media Services*

did spin off as a result of war-time contracts, it could not compensate for the losses due to danger and uncertainties of war upon the high seas.

During this period, the mast trade provided the centerpiece of seacoast New Hampshire's economic life. The huge *pinus strobus* dominated the forests of New Hampshire and yielded two-hundred foot specimens that provided masts for the great sails and rigging on the ships of the Royal Navy. Great care attended the removal of these behemoths from their forest habitats. As the years passed, the source of the giant white pines receded to a distance of twenty to forty miles inland and upcountry from the Great Bay. The large trunks were hauled along straight mast roads. Teams of seventy to eighty oxen dragged the future masts to the water's edge, where the great logs were rafted down the rivers, across the Great Bay, and into Portsmouth.

There, riding at anchor, awaiting their cargo, were large ships specially constructed to accommodate the great bulk of the trees. In the dark recesses of the ships, the trees, shorn of their bark and boughs, were transported to those English shipyards across the Atlantic, where the bounty of New Hampshire's forest was transformed into the smooth masts for the king's warships. The masts bore the sails that carried these vessels across the seven seas to the outposts of the growing British empire. The mast trade served the Royal Navy and focused the economic activity in New Hampshire; the mast trade became increasingly lucrative as each mast commanded the fee of one hundred pounds or better.

Ingenious settlers soon grasped the economic possibilities nature offered. In the mid-seventeenth century enterprising Exeter residents built six sawmills; during the same period ten sawmills were erected in Dover and others were built in Hampton and Portsmouth. Dover accepted lumber in lieu of cash for payment of taxes. The sawmills processed lumber into other products for ship and building construction, including joists, beams, clapboards, spars, yards, riven shingles, staves, barrel tops, and other products. The increasing demand created the need for more sawmills along the shores of the Piscataqua with each passing year. Ships, many of which were built on the Piscataqua, carried the output of the mills to England, the West Indies, southern colonies, Boston, and even illegal ports in Portugal and Spain. The lumber industry encouraged other industries creating activities for sawyers, shipwrights, carpenters, and coopers. The forest and the sea provided a rich catalogue of occupations in those days.

As the mast trade developed, trading patterns favored those families with imperial connections. The navy board in Britain issued contracts to British merchants, who in turn subcontracted orders to merchants known to them in New Hampshire. In *The New England Merchants in the Seventeenth Century*, Harvard historian Bernard Bailyn notes that entrepreneurs such as Thomas Chesley, Peter Coffin, and Richard Waldron of Dover, Robert Wadleigh, Edward Gilman, and the Hiltons of Exeter, Andrew Wiggin and Joseph Chase of Hampton and John Cutt, Bryan Pendleton, John and William Partridge, Walter Abbott and the Wentworths—Samuel and John—all of Portsmouth, profited from the imperial network. These comfortable arrangements came to an abrupt close when the mast trade was subjected to a monopolizing trend which reduced the number of participating merchants. The British Navy began to contract with fewer and fewer English mast suppliers who in turn limited their colonial contacts. Profits were shared with an ever-smaller elite.

At the same time, as a part of the efforts to increase the efficiency of colonial policy, the home government dispatched a surveyor general of the King's Woods to America, charging him with the task of marking all white pines of a prescribed size with three cuts of an axe, creating a pattern, resembling a crude arrow. Only those trees on public property would be subjected to this imperial branding, but the law was not always clear in its distinction between public and private property. The White Pine Act passed by Parliament in 1722 stated that only those white pines outside the towns would be reserved for the navy.

The trade in lumber in the Piscataqua region continued to grow rapidly in the first half of the eighteenth century. Sawmills in the area more than doubled in number during that time so that by 1752 there were two hundred of them turning out a variety of products: furniture, shingles, clapboards, rafters, joists, and firewood.

Old gristmill in Rye, New Hampshire, dating from the late seventeenth century. In 1674 Francis Jeness settled "above ye long stony beach towards the Piscataqua." Jeness and three others engaged John Babson (Barsham) of Great Island to build them a sawmill. From the collection of Bruce E. Ingmire

The concentration of new mills in towns such as Kingston and Nottingham marked the movement of the forest-based economy from the seacoast closer to the source of the supply.

At the same time that sawmills gravitated toward dense forest growth, the shipbuilding industry on the coast enjoyed a steady expansion. While many of the New Hampshire-built ships were smaller sloops or brigs, a large number were of substantial four-hundred-ton weight. The shipwrights continued to come from families like the Bickfords, Millets, and Meserves. They continued to exemplify the habit of New Hampshire residents to use the bounty of the forest and the sea to their commercial advantage.

In the fury of commercial activity, the burning religious questions of the previous generation had become submerged in the pursuit of wealth. Inquisitiveness had been pushed aside by acquisitiveness. Yet the religious ideals had not been totally dismissed. By the turn of the century, the religious questions would be revived and a new enthusiasm would spread throughout all of New England. Today, it is referred to as the Great Awakening. Seacoast New Hampshire, like all of New England, had its two important agendas, commerce and religion, established in these formative years.

The Colcord House, which was built on the same site as Daniel Fowle's first printing office, later demolished. Today yet another house sits on the same site and is owned by the Mark H. Wentworth Home across Pleasant Street.
Courtesy of Strawbery Banke, Inc.

The Wentworth-Coolidge home with lilacs in bloom about 1900. This house was assembled by Benning Wentworth in 1750 in the middle of his term as royal governor of New Hampshire. He moved a (circa) 1710 warehouse and a (circa) 1740 home to the 115-acre site and then added the elegant south wing to create the long asymmetrical edifice that exists today. It was Wentworth's seat of government from 1754 until 1766. The Wentworth-Coolidge House is more typical of mediaeval architecture than the prevailing examples of the Georgian style of Wentworth's day.
Courtesy of the Athenaeum

3

OLIGARCHY AND REVOLUTION

Family had been another hallmark of the Puritan settlement. Throughout the first three-quarters of the eighteenth century one family had assumed dynastic proportions and dominated the province of New Hampshire. For many years prior to 1717, when John Wentworth became lieutenant governor of New Hampshire, the province's government had been combined with Massachusetts. In 1691 New Hampshire had been granted a nominally separate status with its own executive, the lieutenant governor, second to a royal governor who also governed Massachusetts. Power shifted back and forth between Boston and Portsmouth, with political struggles which reflected rifts in America and England between the king and the Parliament and between Anglican and Puritan. In general, adherents of the Puritan cause in the New Hampshire towns of Exeter, Hampton, Dover, and Portsmouth favored the continuation of the subordinate connection with Massachusetts. Anglican communicants, anxious to see the king consolidate his imperial powers, worked for the establishment of a separate royal status for New Hampshire. In 1717 the wishes for a separate status were partially realized with the appointment of Wentworth. They were realized more clearly in 1741 when John Wentworth's son, Benning, was appointed New Hampshire's first resident royal governor.

Benning Wentworth, with very good reason, personified the successful royal governor. A native of New Hampshire and Harvard educated, he belonged to a branch of the Wentworths which had firmly planted them-

*Portrait of young Benning Wentworth
by Joseph Blackburn. Blackburn lived in
Barbados and was a student of John
Singleton Copley. He resided in
Portsmouth in the early 1760s and
painted many of the members of the
oligarchy and their wives.
Courtesy of the New Hampshire
Historical Society and the
Wentworth-Coolidge Museum*

Close-up of the Wentworth-Coolidge home. Wentworth reputedly imported the lilacs, which are among the oldest on the continent. He married his youthful second wife in this home, and she, Martha Hilton Wentworth, married an Englishman, Michael Wentworth, after Benning's death. The house passed to their daughter before it was sold to the Cushing family. Charles Cushing had married into the Sheafe family, long connected with Newcastle history. Courtesy of the Athenaeum

selves in the province and had managed through propitious marriages to establish a network of oligarchical dimensions. Alliances with merchant families such as the Atkinsons, the Sherburnes, and the Warners created a dynasty whose power reached beyond mere local politics into spheres of imperial influence.

One test of wills early in Benning's administration illustrates his astute administrative style. In 1745 the assembly tested his mettle when it refused to admit five delegates from towns to which the governor had recently granted representation in the legislative body. Unlike most royal governors who were dependent upon the assemblies for their salaries, Wentworth, with his independent wealth, played a waiting game with the assembly. After a number of adjournments and prorogations and with the support of the royal government, Wentworth won an unequivocal victory. The assembly acquiesced and seated his five delegates. The stage was set for the next two decades.

Benning's style set the tone for life among Portsmouth's aristocracy until the eve of the Revolution. As his portrait suggests, his manner was haughty and his apparel luxurious. At his fifty-two-room mansion at Little Harbor, he conducted a colonial court with stately dinners of fine cuisine, games, music, and dancing. Longfellow in *Tales of a Wayside Inn* described with poetic license one such evening when the governor, then in his sixties, astonished his guests with the announcement that the Reverend Mr. Arthur Browne, Anglican minister would cap the evening's entertainment by performing the nuptials of the aging chief magistrate and his youthful housekeeper, Martha

Hilton. History has treated Martha as not much more than a poor maid, but she was in fact descended from a founder of the colony and of a good family.

Notwithstanding such an indiscretion, few wished to brook his displeasure, for Benning Wentworth's reach was far. The power of this governor resided not only in his personal wealth and powerful familial relationships; he also maintained close ties with his colony's agents in London, who were ever-scrupulous in guarding his interests. In addition, he held the office of surveyor general of the King's Woods, which put him at the center of new Hampshire's most lucrative enterprise, the trade in masts and lumber and their allied industries. John Thomlinson, New Hampshire's agent in London, had close ties with the Duke of Newcastle, who headed several ministries in the reign of George II. Thomlinson also wielded great influence in the allocation of the coveted contracts for masts, ensuring the dominant role of Benning's brother Mark Hunking Wentworth.

Nepotism flourished in the system, with eight of the governor's relatives serving in the council, while other family relatives both by blood and marriage occupied high positions in the Superior Court, the militia, and served as sheriff, official printer, custom's official, and a variety of other positions which offered all sorts of legal emoluments in the course of service. The governor was even related by marriage to John Huske, a Massachusetts-born member of Parliament in the thick of legislation affecting the colonies.

Surprisingly, there was a positive side to all this. Wentworth proved to be an able administrator who associated

Photograph of the Governor's Council Chamber mantelpiece in the Wentworth-Coolidge House. The photo was taken when the home was owned by the Cushing family of Roxbury, Massachusetts, and before it was sold to the Coolidges in 1885. One theory gives the Dearing family craftsmen credit for the woodwork of the mantelpiece, and the design source is thought to be The Gentleman's and Builder's Repository or Architecture Displayed *by Edward Hoppies, London, editions 1738 and 1748.*
Courtesy of the New Hampshire Historical Society

Recent photograph of the Wentworth-Coolidge home. The Cushing and Coolidge families successively owned the home. Mary Abigail Parsons Coolidge, widow of the last private owner, left it to New Hampshire. It is operated by the State Parks as a historic site.
Courtesy of the Wentworth Coolidge Museum

the best interests of his province along with his own. The colony prospered under his leadership. The assembly was small, there was no charter, and Benning worked effectively with the deputies, leaving many local affairs in their hands. Since the wars with France coincided with many of the years of Wentworth's administration, the crisis atmosphere often helped to engender a spirit of cooperation within the government. The governor went so far in putting the interests of the province ahead of his own that on one occasion when the treasury was depleted, he declined to accept his salary so that other officials might receive theirs. And in an area notorious for smuggling, the governor disregarded illegalities perpetrated by his merchant friends. Even though his mansion overlooked the entrance to Portsmouth Harbor, Wentworth chose to direct his vision elsewhere.

Eventually, as it usually does in history, the truth of Lord Acton's axiom concerning the corrupting influence of excessive power became manifest. With the accession of George III in 1760, a new set of officials moved to the center of the imperial stage, and the Wentworth connections found themselves relegated to the wings. Without recourse to his English power base, Wentworth's influence waned. Worse yet, the Privy Council decided in favor of New York in an old boundary dispute, declaring that the Connecticut River divided New Hampshire from New York, thus rendering Benning's many land grants in the future state of Vermont of questionable authenticity if not actually invalidating them. Further, the Board of Trade requested that the governor step down for misconduct in office. Fortunately for the oligarchy, the Marquis of Rockingham, a very distant cousin, briefly served as prime

Stavers' Tavern in Portsmouth on Court Street was once under the sign of the Earl of Halifax, president of the Board of Trade in the mid-eighteenth century and an aggressive imperialist. Loyalists once met here and planned the strategies that were used to thwart the patriots. During the American Revolution the tavern was renamed the William Pitt Tavern and, under that name, is in 1989 a part of Strawbery Banke, Inc. Pitt was perceived as more of a friend of the colonists and was a more appro-

priate name choice than Halifax.

Bartholomew Stavers, who operated from his father's stables, was a post rider for Daniel Fowel's New Hampshire Gazette. *It may very well be that Stavers, the nefarious Paul Wentworth, and Benjamin Thompson met and directed loyalists and agents of the crown. All were eventually listed as loyalists and banned from the country. Paul Wentworth was no relation to the governor. Later Paul Wentworth became the British Secret Service's case officer for Dr.*

Edward Bancroft. Bancroft, who was Benjamin Franklin's secretary in Paris, secretly worked for the British Secret Service. While Franklin was minister to France working to formalize the Franco-American alliance, Bancroft reported Franklin's daily maneuvers directly to Paul Wentworth, who frequently went to Paris to get the reports.
Courtesy of the University of New Hampshire Media Services and Gary Sampson

minister at the time, and he arranged that the old governor should be succeeded by his nephew, the personable John Wentworth.

The new, young governor enjoyed only a brief honeymoon in Portsmouth. As the crisis in relations with the mother country escalated with the passage of the Townshend Acts and the Tea Act, he found himself boxed in between an increasingly militant London government and an assembly grown restive and more belligerent in defending its rights. With the coming of peace with France, the demand for masts decreased. The pre-eminence of the seacoast and its towns dating back to the seventeenth century suffered eclipse with the rise of new communities in the Merrimack and Connecticut River valleys. The settlers were from Massachusetts and Connecticut, and their traditions and values differed from

those of the older inhabitants. The stability which characterized the years of his uncle's era gave way to a time of growing volatility. Challenges to the governor's authority came with increasing frequency; in 1773 the assembly disregarded his wishes and organized a Committee of Correspondence for the purpose of exchanging information with other provincial governments. In December of that same year, the Boston Tea Party erupted as a direct result of the colonists' opposition to Parliament's tax on tea. When the British government retaliated with the Coercive Acts, abrogating the Massachusetts Charter and closing the Port of Boston, tensions increased. Towns began to pass inflammatory resolutions condemning the British Parliament's attempts to tax Americans without their consent; the old seacoast communities, including Dover, Portsmouth, Hampton,

Gen. John Sullivan House in Durham is an eighteenth-century residence. This photo was taken in 1908. Sullivan was of Irish descent and became a prominent general during the American Revolution. Both he and his brother, Daniel, were approached numerous times by the British in regard to deserting the American cause. Daniel died but John served as governor of the state. Thomas F. Reid is the present owner of the premises.
Courtesy of
Mr. and Mrs. George Frost Sawyer

The Stone Store was located off 1989s Market Street in Portsmouth and was near the former site of Pres. John Cutt's house in the seventeenth century. It is the pre-Revolutionary site of the building where the customs official Eleazer Russell, Jr., used to smoke up the room in which he was to handle documents. He always handled the papers with instruments. This was the aging and finicky bachelor's attempt to control the spread of smallpox. He thought the disease was brought by each ship to the port and that the smoke would arrest the germs. Russell was the great-grandson of Joshua Moodey, the well known Puritan minister of Portsmouth. He was the grandson of Jonathan Russell, minister of Barnstead on Cape Cod.
Courtesy of the Athenaeum

Slave quarters at General Sullivan's house in Durham are no longer in existence. The young man at the door is George Sawyer as a boy of about six. Courtesy of Mr. and Mrs. George Frost Sawyer

and Exeter, concurred in their opposition to British policy. Governor Wentworth's efforts to control the assembly met with a recalcitrance he found difficult to comprehend.

In the summer of 1774, the New Hampshire committee of correspondence invited each town in the colony to send two representatives to the Provincial Congress. Once convened, the group chose Nathaniel Folsom of Exeter and John Sullivan of Durham to serve as Delegates to the Continental Congress scheduled to meet at Philadelphia in the autumn. These acts marked the beginning of the formation of those extra-legal bodies, which in time, with the disintegration of the old regime, would become the legal government of the new state. The Committee of Correspondence in Portsmouth was led by none other than the deceased Benning Wentworth's aging brother, Hunking Wentworth. Long distanced from the affluence of Benning, Hunking represented the same line but more egalitarian politics.

Perhaps the most explosive event witnessed by the seacoast area during the Revolution took place on December 14 and 15, 1774, when about four hundred men from Portsmouth, Newcastle, and Rye marched upon Fort William and Mary, located in Newcastle at the entrance to Portsmouth Harbor. The attack had been precipitated partly by the arrival in Portsmouth the previous day of that indefatigable horseman, Paul Revere, at the house of Hunking Wentworth. He brought with him a communication stating that the British government had forbidden the exportation of gunpowder and military stores to America and that troops soon would arrive to reinforce those at the New Hampshire fort. Samuel Cutts, the young mastermind of the Portsmouth Committee of Correspondence, summoned his fellow patriot conspirators, who decided that the ammunition must be removed from the fort. Rallied by their leaders, four hundred men

Durham Frost's House with the rear ell, thought to date as early as 1648. If corroborating data could be found, it would be older than the Jackson House in Portsmouth.
Courtesy of
Mr. and Mrs. George Frost Sawyer

Interior of the Frost House with paintings now the property of the Portsmouth Athenaeum. The paintings of family members are displayed in the Copley Research Library.
Courtesy of
Mr. and Mrs. George Frost Sawyer

marched to Newcastle, where they demanded the surrender of the fort. Captain Cochran and his five-man garrison offered token resistance, a few shots were exchanged, and the fort capitulated. About one hundred barrels of gunpowder were transported up the Piscataqua to Durham, and the following day John Sullivan of that town led a second assault on the fort, and the small arms and lighter cannon were spirited away. This proved to be the only military action on New Hampshire soil throughout the Revolution, for the Granite State was the only one of the original thirteen that saw no battle fought within its borders.

When the second Provincial Congress met in Exeter in January 1775, deputies called upon the towns to take heed of the growing danger and to prepare to defend themselves against a possible invasion. Government was reduced to the local level, a development not entirely unusual, for New Hampshire towns had always enjoyed considerable autonomy. Functions of that central government that did continue to exist were increasingly assumed by the Provincial Congress as the authority of the governor and his council dissipated.

Royal Gov. John Wentworth made one final attempt to reestablish his authority in the spring of 1775, when he convened the old assembly. In order to ensure a loyal majority, he granted to three towns in the Connecticut Valley region the right to send delegates to the assembly, believing they would return men who would ensure him a majority. The assembly refused to cooperate and excluded the new representatives. On a June evening, one of these gentlemen, John Fenton, dined with the governor and his wife at their residence on Pleasant Street. Learning of his presence, citizens assembled outside the house and demanded that Fenton surrender to the mob. Fenton complied when a cannon appeared, its barrel pointed ominously at the front door. Wentworth, his patience tried and his fears for the safety of his wife and infant son heightened, fled that night to Fort William and Mary, where he was protected by the British frigate *Scarborough*. At the end of the summer, he departed for Boston aboard

the *Scarborough*. Royal government in New Hampshire had ended.

In place of the old regime, the Provincial Congress gradually assumed the responsibilities and authority of the government; what had been extra-legal became legal. Exeter became the seat of government, displacing the elegant seaport that had served for so long as the center for New Hampshire's economic, social, and political life but which was heavily identified with the old regime and Tory sympathies. The egalitarian impulse of revolution caused the Provincial Congress to decrease property qualifications for its members and to grant the franchise to all tax-paying legal inhabitants. Doors were opened to inland towns hitherto denied representation, further decreasing the dominant role enjoyed by the seacoast throughout the colonial period. Later, New Hampshire adopted a new constitution, and the old colony became a new state.

Though Portsmouth may have ceased to be the capital, it remained the focus of Loyalism. Those whose hearts and minds remained with King George III were men who had held their heads high in offices under the direction of the crown. Some, however, like the last royal governor's own father, Mark Hunking Wentworth, and Theodore Atkinson, Sr., the royal governor's uncle by marriage, eventually turned to the revolutionary cause. Both aging men were apparently shocked by the young governor's hasty marriage and the subsequent birth of his only child. Both men were also distrustful of the governor's treacherous accomplice, Paul Wentworth. In the hinterland, people of humbler origin sometimes espoused the royal cause, but seacoast Tories tended to belong to the old aristocracy. Loyalists worshipped at queen's chapel and cherished their Anglican association. In exile the former royal governor and his lady went to Nova Scotia, where he served as chief official.

As long as the old guard did not flaunt improper political opinions, the new government was loathe to prosecute. The former court printer, Daniel Fowle, quietly passed his presses to former apprentices who espoused the revolutionary cause. Some patriots, including Gen. John Sulivan, continued to voice their suspicions. In October 1775, he wrote to George Washington about "that infernal crew of Tories, who have endeavored to prevent fortifying this harbor, walk the streets here with impunity,

Walbach Tower in Newcastle was obscured by the Farnesworth Battery, built in 1897. The martello-type fortification was erected in 1814 during the War of 1812. These circular masonry forts first appeared on the island of Corsica and became popular during the Napoleonic Wars. Colonel Walbach was the military officer in charge of the fort. Courtesy of Strawbery Banke, Inc.

and will, with a sneer, tell the people in the streets that all our liberty-poles will soon be converted to gallows." To prevent the realization of such a dire prediction, newly created committees of safety assumed as part of their duties the surveillance of all suspected Loyalists. Before the Revolution ended, some of these unfortunates suffered incarceration in an Exeter jail. In 1778, with the passage of an act of banishment, almost half of those who left the state lived in Portsmouth.

Even though there were no battles within the boundaries of New Hampshire, many of the sons of the state saw service in the great battles of the war. In the spirit of enthusiasm that infused all patriots in the early days of the Revolution, almost ten thousand volunteers from southern New Hampshire marched to the environs of Boston at the time of the battles of Lexington and Concord. Later that year when the Continental Congress decided that only a regular, standing army could defeat the British, they created the Continental Army and appointed George Washington commander-in-chief. New Hampshire's legislature responded by authorizing three regiments totaling two thousand soldiers. Sons of the Granite State served

with particular distinction at Bunker Hill, in the invasion of Canada, and at the Battle of Saratoga. An outstanding contribution came when Gen. John Stark, commanding New Hampshire troops at Bennington, won a singular victory against General Burgoyne's invasion forces.

In addition to serving in the military, outstanding residents of the seacoast played major political roles. William Whipple of Portsmouth and Josiah Bartlett of Kingston signed the Declaration of Independence. Nicholas Gilman of Exeter and John Langdon of Portsmouth helped to draft the United States Constitution. Tobias Lear, a native of Portsmouth and descended from original land grantees of the Piscataqua, became General Washington's trusted personal secretary.

When Concord became the state capitol in 1809, the seacoast's long dominance of provincial and state affairs came to an end. As more settlers poured into the interior of the state, the center of population, as well as the center of commercial and political activity, shifted to the northwest. The legacy of nearly two centuries of leadership remained with the seacoast and its former capital cities.

John Langdon was born in Portsmouth, New Hampshire, on June 26, 1741. By the time of the Revolution, he was a person of influence. He participated in the attack upon Fort William and Mary in 1774, when the fort was attacked and military supplies were forcibly removed. During the Revolution, he served in the Continental Congress, amassed a fortune as a privateer, and organized and financed the expedition from new Hampshire, led by Gen. John Stark that resulted in the American victory at Bennington, Vermont. As a militia commander, he was present at Burgoyne's surrender at Saratoga.

After the Revolution he served as a delegate to the Constitutional Convention and in 1789 entered the U.S. Senate. He was the first president pro tempore of the U.S. Senate. Starting as a Federalist, he switched to the Republican party and became associated with Thomas Jefferson. After he left the Senate, he served as governor of New Hampshire.

In 1777, the year of the Saratoga campaign, he married the sixteen-year-old daughter of John Sherburne, Elizabeth. Their elaborate home on Pleasant Street remains one of the most splendid in the city. Langdon died in 1819. His descendants, the Thomas Elwyn family, gave many gifts to the citizens of Portsmouth, including Langdon Park, the former hospital grounds, and the Urban Forestry land. Courtesy of the University of New Hampshire Media Services

The Langdon barn in Newington, New Hampshire, was on a summer estate of the Langdon family and was recently demolished.
Photo by Dorothy Watson

A photograph of the Ledges in Durham taken in 1917. At present it is the home of Mr. and Mrs. George Frost Sawyer. Courtesy of Mr. and Mrs. George Frost Sawyer

The garden in back of the John Langdon House on Pleasant Street in Portsmouth. Today this garden is meticulously managed by Mr. Gary Wetzel, under of the auspices of the Society for the Preservation of New England Antiquities. Courtesy of Strawbery Banke, Inc.

The Walker Farm in Durham. The property was owned by the James Chamberlins and is in 1989 the Mill Pond Center. Courtesy of Mr. and Mrs. George Frost Sawyer

Newmarket Road Bridge across Oyster River in Durham with the Old Mill on the right. This was the earliest center of the town, then called Oyster River. The miller was the first victim of the Oyster River massacre in 1692, which eventually took one hundred lives.
Courtesy of
Mrs. and Mrs. George Frost Sawyer

Raits Court off Vaughan Street in Portsmouth, New Hampshire, and the 1750 Assembly House, built by Michael Whidden. Later it was divided into two units which were placed across the street from each other. Before it became private dwellings, the building served as the social gathering place for the well-to-do in the Revolutionary period. In 1789 George Washington attended a reception in the building.
Courtesy of the Athenaeum

Turn of the century view of the Wentworth Gardener House (center) in the South End of Portsmouth. The cupola of the South End Meeting House can be seen at left. The South End Meeting House was rebuilt at the end of the nineteenth century and is now the Children's Museum. The house of Tobias Lear, private secretary to General George Washington, is located to the extreme left of the photo.
Courtesy of the Athenaeum

The Wentworth Gardner House was built in the mid-eighteenth century by the wife of Mark Hunking Wentworth, Elizabeth Rindge Wentworth, for her son Thomas, the youngest brother of the last royal governor, John Wentworth. Later Maj. Wiliam Gardner, a revolutionary patriot, purchased the home, and his family owned it for years. Charles Dale was instrumental in saving the house when the Metropolitan Museum of New York threatened to move the entire building to New York and place it in Central Park. Today the house has a rusticated facade that is different from the clapboard seen here.
From the collection of Bruce E. Ingmire

The Meserve House in Portsmouth's North End was situated across from Raits Court and, like so many houses in that section, was built by Michael Whidden. It was occupied by George Meserve, who was appointed but did not serve as the tax collector during the Stamp Act crisis of 1765. Later Daniel Webster lived in the house with his bride.
From the collection of Bruce E. Ingmire

A back view of the Raits Court buildings. Courtesy of Strawbery Banke, Inc.

Bosen Allen's House on Newcastle's riverfront. Note the old well. The home was torn down at the time of the First World War.
Courtesy of Strawbery Banke, Inc.

Bosen Allen's House was located on the Piscataqua and was an eighteenth-century building. Boatswain Allen is supposed to have served with Commodore John Paul Jones, but many people have thought Allen was more myth than matter.
Courtesy of Strawbery Banke, Inc.

A postal card view of the Wendell House on Pleasant Street in Portsmouth. From the collection of Bruce E. Ingmire

Wendell House, whose last occupant was Mrs. Evelyn Wendell, who passed away the summer of 1988, when this book was being written. The arrangements involving the home require that a family member named Wendell come into possession of the home.
Courtesy of the Athenaeum

*Interior of the Wendell House in the
early 1900s. Mrs. Barrett Wendell lived
in this house at that time. She purchased
the Warner House and saw to its
preservation. Her husband wrote the*
Puritan Priest.
Courtesy of the Athenaeum

The Salter House near the South Mill Pond entrance was the home of Capt. Titus Salter and later of Henry P. Salter. From the collection of Bruce E. Ingmire

More recent photo of the Parsonage at Newington, New Hampshire. Courtesy of the Langdon Library, Newington, New Hampshire

The Parsonage was built in 1710 and first occupied by the Rev. Joseph Adams, uncle of Pres. John Adams. Courtesy of the Langdon Library, Newington, New Hampshire

St. John's Episcopal Church in Portsmouth. This brick church replaced an earlier wooden structure, known as the Queen's Chapel, which served as the place of worship for Portsmouth's colonial elite. Royal Gov. Benning Wentworth is buried in a vault on the site. George Washington attended a service in the Queen's Chapel.
Courtesy of the Athenaeum

The interior of St. John's Curch showing the trompe l'oeil *painting that creates the illusion of a third dimension.*
Courtesy of the Athenaeum

Sheafe's Warehouse was restored and moved a few feet to its present location in Prescott Park.
Courtesy of the Athenaeum

Sheafe's Warehouse before it was moved to its present site. The wooden warehouse is a relic of eighteenth-century waterborne commerce.
Courtesy of the Athenaeum

The "Old Jail" on Islington Street was built in 1782 after a fire destroyed the earlier prison on Prison Lane, which was located on what is now Porter lane. This jail was abandoned when the new one was built on Pennhallow Street in 1891.
Islington took its name from the creek that emptied into the North Mill Pond and where a gristmill was located. A few homes were built at the site, and a glade called McDonough's led to the area. The quaint romantic interlude was called Islington. Nothing is left to remind one of that lost era.
Courtesy of the Athenaeum

The Liberty Pole, now a flagpole, and Sheafe's Warehouse. Sheafe's is thought to have been built about 1705 as the area turned into a more commercial section of Portsmouth, replacing the wharfs lost when Newcastle became a town in 1693.
Courtesy of the Athenaeum

The State House was built in 1758 and housed the Governor's Council, the House of Representatives, and the Court of Common Law. The building was moved to Court Street in 1836, when a Greek Revival courthouse was built to replace the aging building and to open up the throat of Congress Street. It is shown here about 1935. In the days before electric wires spanned city thoroughfares, moving a house, especially one of half-timber frame, was a relatively easy task. Unfortunately today the presence of electrical wires makes moving buildings a costly endeavor, Inadvertently, concern for electric wires prevents salvaging older wooden architecture by relocation.
Courtesy of the Athenaeum

One-third of the State House in 1988 at Strawbery Banke, Inc.
From the collection of Bruce E. Ingmire

Daniel Fowel occupied this office on the corner of Pleasant and Howard from the time he first arrived in Portsmouth in 1756 until about 1762. It was here that the first book in New Hampshire was printed and the first number of the New Hampshire Gazette *was issued on October 7, 1756. From this site numerous apprentices ran to meet ships arriving from Europe. The ship's captain collected newspapers from London and other continental ports which provided the printer with his latest "intelligences." Fowel, like any colonial printer, set his type from the chronological events listed in the newspapers thus collected. When King George II died in November of 1760, it was not until the first week of January that the* New Hampshire Gazette *was able to report the news and the colony was able to mourn the old king and salute the new king, George III.*
Courtesy of Strawbery Banke, Inc.

The Deer Street Tavern in the North End of Portsmouth was built about 1705 and was presumably a haunt of the opposition party that waited in the wings for the Wentworths to end their rule. Like so many other buildings, it was torn down.
Courtesy of the Athenaeum

Manning House, at the corner of Manning Place and Marcy (Water) Street in Portsmouth, was built by Capt. Thomas Manning in the early eighteenth century. Manning was the first to use the name Congress Street instead of King Street in proclaiming the end of British rule after the Declaration of Independence was read in Portsmouth from the Old State House. His wife is buried in the tiny Pleasant Street Cemetery.
Courtesy of the Athenaeum

The Puddle Dock Wentworth House on Manning Street in Portsmouth was taken down in the 1920s. It was built by Thomas Daniel, the husband of Bridget Cutts Daniel Graffort. Later, Edward Cranfield purchased it. Then he traded it for a property owned by Samuel Wentworth on Great Island. Samuel brewed and sold beer there. Parts of the interior of the home were sold and were preserved at Winturthur and the Metropolitan Museum of Art in New York. Courtesy of the Athenaeum

The home of the Colonel Pierce family about 1882 on Lower Congress, just below today's Kearsarge Building. It was built by William Sheafe about 1785, and was purchased in 1839 by Colonel Pierce, the son of John Pierce, who built the Pierce mansion at Haymarket Square and who owned the insurance company which built the Athenaeum. This picture shows the landscape after a winter snow has receded. Courtesy of the Athenaeum

*State Street and the Tredick House,
which was situated where the Rockingham Court House was built in 1891. In
1989 it is the site of the Piscataqua
Bank parking lot and drive-up window.
Courtesy of Strawbery Banke, Inc.*

The Gilman House in Exeter in 1908. This building housed the State Treasury during the American Revolution. Recently an early copy of the Declaration of Independence was discovered in the building. Nicholas Gilman, delegate to the Constitutional Convention, lived in the house. Currently it is the headquarters of the Society of the Cincinnati in New Hampshire.
Courtesy of Sandusky and the New Hampshire Society of the Cincinnati

A 1988 view of Exeter's Gilman House. Photo by Paul Farrell

The Fourth Academy Building, Phillips Exeter Academy. This building, designed by Cram and Ferguson, was dedicated in 1915. Phillips Exeter Academy was founded in 1781 by John Phillips (1719-1795), a philanthropist, public servant, and businessman. One of the leading private preparatory schools in the country, it counts among its famous graduates Daniel Webster, Edward Everett, Franklin Pierce, Robert Lincoln, and several writers including Booth Tarkington, John Knowles, and John Irving.
Photo by Paul Farrell

Governor Plummer residence in Epping, New Hampshire.
Courtesy of the Epping Historical Society

The United States destroyer Brooks. *This photo was taken on July 5, 1924, as the ship lay on the rocks at Fort Point near the entrance of Portsmouth Harbor following a storm in which the* Brooks *ran aground.*
Couretsy of Rye Historical Society

4
SHIPWRIGHTS TO SUBMARINE ENGINEERS

As a result of the foundation in commercial ship-building during the seventeenth century, the production of naval warships followed logically. The numerous islands in the Piscataqua provided strategic sites for naval construction. Badger's Island in Kittery, Maine, played host to the shipwrights who in 1690 constructed the *Falkland*, a large, fifty-four gun frigate, for the British Royal Navy. In the eighteenth century, Badger's Island became the property of John Langdon, revolutionary leader, and under his direction and that of Capt. John Paul Jones, America's first naval hero, three naval vessels were built and launched. Jones at times resided in Portsmouth during the construction of the warships.

The first of these, the *Raleigh*, was built in the remarkably short time of sixty days. Much to Langdon's indignation, the ship remained at anchor, minus its guns for over a year. The *Raleigh* finally put to sea in August 1777, and the following year after a seven-hour battle with two British frigates off the Maine coast, it was taken by the British and suffered the indignity of "impressment" into the Royal Navy.

The second Continental Naval vessel constructed on the Piscataqua enjoyed a more illustrious career; the *Ranger*, captained by the intrepid John Paul Jones, sailed

Frigates Portsmouth *and* Saratoga *in Portsmouth Harbor.*
Courtesy of the Athenaeum

Lighthouse at Fort Point, Great Island, Newcastle. This site at the mouth of the Piscataqua and on Great Island has been a military installation since the days of the 1652 creation of Portsmouth, New Hampshire. The first lighthouse was built under the administration of John Wentworth in 1771 after the royal governor made an impassioned plea that the Assembly either build a lighthouse or at least pay for a lantern to be hung from the mast that supports the flagstaff at the "Castle."
From the Sweetser Collection; courtesy of Mrs. and Mrs. William Warren

from Portsmouth on November 1, 1777, charged with carrying the dispatches to France containing the momentous news of General Burgoyne's defeat at Saratoga just two weeks before. The American victory at Saratoga contributed to the French decision to sign a treaty of alliance with the infant republic. After the arrival in France, the *Ranger* sailed to Quiberon Bay, and a French naval vessel fired the first salute ever paid the American flag. According to William Saltonstall's *Ports of the Piscataqua*, tradition has it that this flag had been "stitched by the patriotic ladies of Portsmouth who used silk taken from their best gowns."

The third vessel, the *America*, largest of the three ships built on the Piscataqua, carried seventy-four guns and, in addition to these weapons of destruction, also bore exquisitely carved figures of Neptune, Mars, and Wisdom, as well as other allegorical representations. This magnificent ship never saw service in the Continental Navy; after its completion, it was turned over to the French in partial payment of war debts. Captured by the British in

1794, it was still in the service of the Royal Navy in 1846. It is important to remember, as Saltonstall observed in his *Ports of the Piscataqua*, that all these ships, though built in Portsmouth, owed their existence to the whole Piscataqua region. Not only did the area contribute its timber, but the skills of craftsmen and mariners drawn from the drowned local towns, combined in the creation of sails, cordage, fittings, and fixtures for these superb sailing ships of, first the British Royal Navy, then the Continental Navy, and eventually the United States Navy.

Once the young republic recovered from the immediate impact of the Revolution, the economy resumed its growth. The seacoast region still exported those products which had been the mainstay of its colonial trade: fish and timber products. However, imports including salt, coal, rum and sugar, unfortunately exceeded exports, leaving the seacoast with an unfavorable balance of trade. There was a short period of prosperity in the 1790s but the years until 1820 marked general economic decline.

In the second and third decades of the nineteenth century, things began to change when the cotton trade added to the volume of commerce of the Piscataqua. Ships from this region picked up cotton at southern ports such as Savannah and Mobile and transported it to England, where it went to the textile mills of the Midlands. Later, when New England developed its own textile industry, ships brought Southern cotton to the North.

The ships engaging in those widespread activities were locally built in the ports of the Piscataqua. Towns such as Exeter, Durham, and South Berwick, which have since lost their association with the sea, produced brigs, schooners, and sloops as well as square-rigged, three-masted vessels. This diverse activity gradually decelerated and had disappeared long before the Civil War. The inability of the hinterland to produce desirable exports in large quantities and the expanding railroad facilities brought the demise of the river connection among those towns that ringed Great Bay, the Piscataqua, and its tributaries. The ships that had been built by entrepreneurs such as Eliph-

alet Ladd of Exeter and Portsmouth and Joseph Coe of Durham could be seen only as paintings lining the walls of sanctuaries such as Portsmouth Athenaeum.

Many merchant ships and privateers slid down the ways, contributing to the prosperity of Portsmouth and its environs. Economic stagnation following the War of 1812 remained until the late 1840s and 1850s when events like the California Gold Rush contributed to a resurgence in New England ship construction. Shipyards such as those of Fernald and Pettigrew and George Raynes soon launched the swift, glamorous clipper ships and packet ships so important to that era. The graceful, fast-moving ships sailed the seven seas. The most famous of the Portsmouth built clippers, the *Nightingale*, had a varied career carrying passengers to the London Exposition of 1850, slaves from Africa, and prospectors to California and Australia. Involvement in illegal trade underscores a dark side to the history of the legendary clippers. Clippers not only carried illegal slaves, but shanghaied Chinese through Puget Sound to work on the transcontinental railroad, and the clipper

The U.S.S. Constitution *served the country well during the War of 1812, remaining active until the 1850s, when it returned to Portsmouth to be refitted. After Dr. Oliver Wendell Holmes wrenched the heart of American children with his poem to save the warship, it was covered over with a superstructure and served as a museum on the Piscataqua. In 1897, at its approaching century launching date, the naval secretary, in a more fitting tribute, ordered the ship restored to its original state. It sailed to its present site in Charlestown, Massachusetts, on September 21, 1897. Courtesy of the Athenaeum*

Brenda carried opium from India to China. Even the proper Victorians profited from the tempting illicit trade.

In stark contrast to the romantic clippers, the Piscataqua region also produced the unique, sturdy, and dependable gundalow. The name is thought to be a corruption of the Italian canal vehicle, the gondola. This jack-of-all-trades of the Great Bay region evolved from the small seventeenth-century ferries that English settlers first piloted upon the Piscataqua. By the mid-nineteenth century, the flat, long scows were the backbone of the shipping trade on the river system. They were fully decked, carried a lateen sail, and were steered by a permanent rudder rigged to a wheel. The sail was fixed to a mast that could be lowered so that the ship could pass beneath the stationary bridges that spanned the numerous rivers comprising the system of tributaries to the Piscataqua River. These ships were familiar sights as they serviced the inland towns of Durham, Dover, Newmarket, Exeter, and Somersworth. Ideally suited to navigate the shallows in the Squamscot, Oyster, Lamprey, Bellamy, Cocheco, and Salmon Falls rivers, the gundalows carried hay, lumber, bricks, flour, and livestock down the river. The ships sailed back upriver with cargos of coal and cotton destined to go to mills like the Cocheco Manufacturing Company in Dover. Gundalows brought the finished products back down the river and coasting vessels called schooners then carried the textiles to Boston. A shoreline spectator during the 1880s would be hard pressed to keep an accurate daily count of the hundreds of coasting vessels and transatlantic ships tacking to Boston and beating to Portland past the mouth of the Piscataqua.

The gundalows may not have generated the excitement of the ocean-going clippers or men-of-war, but for years they were the backbone of commerce from the Great Bay and inland towns to the seacoast and beyond. Eventually the "iron horse" and, in the modern day, the diesel truck have replaced those working vessels of bygone eras. The river transportation remains important today. Huge cargo, tanker and container ships, behemoths compared to the ships of yesterday, now ply the Piscataqua.

John Paul Jones' legacy of military shipbuilding resulted in the founding of the United States navy yard at Portsmouth in 1800. Then Secretary of the Navy Benjamin Stoddard purchased Fernald's Island in Maine, and with the coming of the War of 1812, ships were soon docking at the Portsmouth naval Shipyard for repairs. Although actually located in Kittery, Maine, the shipyard took its name from the customs district in which it was located. The *Washington*, a seventy-four gun ship, became the first U.S. Naval vessel built in the new shipyard and was launched in 1815. Operations increased, keeping pace with technology, and the introduction of the steam frigate *Franklin*, built in 1854, necessitated reconstruction of the 1838 shiphouse, Building 53. The cavernous structure, the largest shiphouse in the United States, was called the Franklin House and dominated the skyline of the yard until fire devoured it early in this century.

With the outbreak of the Civil War, the activity at the Portsmouth Naval Shipyard accelerated; between the years 1861 and 1865, twenty-six ships were added to the Union Navy. The most famous was the *Kearsarge*, a sloop of nine guns which was launched in 1861. The *Kearsarge* sank the

notorious Confederate raider *Alabama* off the coast of France in 1864. The yard grew in size with the addition of Seavey's Island, and even though production slowed with the arrival of peace, such local magnates as brewer Frank Jones kept the yard open during the 1870s, when he served in the United States Congress. When William Chandler from the state capital in Concord served as secretary of the navy in the administration of Chester Alan Arthur (1881-1885), he proved to be another forceful advocate of the Portsmouth Naval Shipyard. Later, Theodore Roosevelt, first as assistant secretary of the navy and then as president, advocated naval policies that not only assured bustling production but saw to improvement of navigation on the river by the removal of Henderson's Point and the fortification of the entire Piscataqua harbor entrance. Henderson's Point had been a notorious navigation impediment, known to local captains headed upriver as "Pull, yank and be damned."

The yard added a diplomatic dimension to its history in 1905 when, at the invitation of President Theodore Roosevelt, the delegates of Russia and Japan met in the old Supply Building to hammer out the details of the agreements that ended their conflict in the Far East. The negotiations, accompanied by much socializing in Portsmouth and Newcastle, bore fruit with the signing of the Treaty of Portsmouth on September 5, 1905. For a brief time, the Piscataqua had been the diplomatic capital of the world. Another unusual event had occurred seven years earlier during the Spanish-American War, when Spanish prisoners had been incarcerated at the yard. A naval prison, built in 1908 to accommodate similar situations, was another of Theodore Roosevelt's naval innovations.

As World War I approached, the research, construction, and maintenance of a U.S. submarine force became the predominant mission of the Portsmouth Naval Shipyard. The first submarine was completed there in 1914; it was 165 feet long and weighed 456 tons. During the war, the keels of six submarines were laid there, and by the end of the conflict, almost six thousand employees were employed in submarine research and developement.

When Franklin Roosevelt moved into the White House in 1933, he brought to the office of the presidency experience as assistant secretary of the navy. Alarmed by the rise of dictatorships in Europe, the second Roosevelt also asked Congress for increased appropriations for the navy. As a result, work at the Portsmouth Naval Shipyard increased its tempo, and soon more submarines joined the fleet. Among them was the *Squalus*, which was commissioned in 1939. In a trial run in May of that year, the *Squalus* sank off the Isles of Shoals. The sister ship of the *Squalus* was the first ship to reach the stricken sub. Although twenty-three of the crew died, the remaining thirty-three survived. As spectators who lived on the shores of the Atlantic in Rye and Hampton watched, the ship was raised and towed to Portsmouth. Repaired and recommissioned as the *Sailfish*, the submarine earned a distinguished record during World War II in the Pacific, sinking a number of Japanese vessels including an aircraft carrier. The superstructure of the *Sailfish* remains at the yard as a memorial to the history of the legendary submarine.

During the war, nearly 2,200 army soldiers were stationed in the Twenty-second Army Artillery Corps, which manned the Harbor Entrance Defense Command at Forts Constitution, Stark, Dearborn, and Camp Langdon. Having

George Raynes was one of Portsmouth's principal shipbuilders. He purchased the North Mill shipyard that had once been owned by the Merserve family. The Raynes shipyard produced the clipper ships of the 1840s and the 1850s. Among the ships were the Sea Serpent, *the* Witch of the Wave, *the* Coeur de Lion, *and the* Webster, *which at 1,727 tons was the largest ship launched on the Piscataqua to the date of 1853. A record maker, the* Sea Serpent *once sailed from Hong Kong to New York in 78 days, which for that time was astonishingly quick.*
Courtesy of the Athenaeum

View of the Franklin Shiphouse at the Portsmouth naval Shipyard. It burned about 1939.
Courtesy of the Athenaeum

become familiar with the port while taking refuge in Little Harbor on cruises north to Campobello, President Franklin Roosevelt visited the yard in August of 1940. The work force grew steadily for the next five years; in 1945 there were twenty thousand civilian workers at the yard. Seventy-nine submarines, many of which saw active service, were built at Portsmouth during the war years, and British and Free-French submarines received overhauling there. Among the latter was the *Surcouf,* which, after departing Portsmouth, disappeared under mysterious circumstances. Altogether, the Portsmouth Naval Shipyard made a great contribution to the Allied victory.

After the war's conclusion, Portsmouth turned to the construction of nuclear submarines. Among this class of ships was the *Abraham Lincoln,* weighing more than six thousand tons. The *Albacore,* an experimental submarine built in 1952-1953, had a distinguished career and became a local tourist attraction, now permanently situated in the former Cutts Cove. In 1983 the U.S.S. *Portsmouth* was commissioned at the yard and was the first ship to be commissioned there since 1969, and thus, after two centuries, the Portsmouth Naval Shipyard continues to play an important role in the seacoast and in the defense of the nation. In fact, it maintains a seafaring tradition that goes back to the original English settlers.

The U.S.S. Galena *in 1877. Galena is the town in Illinois where General Grant lived. Courtesy of Strawbery Banke, Inc.*

The U.S.S. Lancaster *in 1880. Courtesy of Strawbery Banke, Inc.*

A December 1906 view of the William Davenport *arriving at Newmarket. Courtesy of Newmarket Historical Society*

The Portsmouth riverfront about 1890 looking up the river from Ceres Street at what was the old fishing market. Courtesy of the Athenaeum

Ferry headed to the "ferry landing" at the Ceres Street waterfront in Portsmouth, about 1910. Ceres Street was so named because the brick buildings which once sat directly on the water's edge were warehouses storing grain for export.
From the collection of Bruce E. Ingmire

Portsmouth's riverfront before the erection of the Memorial Bridge. Notice the old wharfs. St. John's Episcopal Church is seen in the center, and the Franklin Shiphouse is seen in the left-hand distance. Courtesy of the Athenaeum

Portsmouth riverfront, in 1890, with a number of coasting schooners in evidence.
Courtesy of the Athenaeum

The ships of the Greeley Expedition of 1884.
Courtesy of Strawbery Banke, Inc.

A view of a section of the Portsmouth Naval Shipyard taken about the time of the Peace Conference in 1905. The conference completed its work with the signing of the Treaty of Portsmouth, which ended a conflict beween Russia and Japan.
Courtesy of Robert A. Whitehouse

Guns captured from the Spanish cruisers Viscaya *and* Maria Teresa, *July 3, 1898, and displayed at the Portsmouth Shipyard.*
Courtesy of Robert A. Whitehouse

Spanish prisoners washed dishes near their barracks, seen in the background. They were put to work around the yard for the two months they were incarcerated.
Courtesy of the Athenaeum

These Spanish prisoners were captured in Cuba during the Spanish American War in 1898 and brought to Portsmouth on the ships City of St. Louis, *the* City of Rome, *and the* Harvard. *The men stayed in Portsmouth for two months.*
Courtesy of the Athenaeum

Spanish prisoners were transported on barges to Seavey's Island. Two other prison ships that came into the port were the U.S.S. Southery *and the U.S.S.* Topeka. *The chief bo's'n for the prison ships was William Lowell Hill.*
Courtesy of the Athenaeum

Departure of the prisoners for Santander, Spain, September 12, 1898. About thirty of the captives died while they were at the Shipyard.
Courtesy of the Athenaeum

One of the ships of Theodore Roosevelt's Great White Fleet docked at the Portsmouth Naval Shipyard.
Courtesy of Robert A. Whitehouse

Henderson's Point formerly extended into the river just opposite Pierce Island, Portsmouth. It was destroyed along with other islands at the mouth of the river in the period of the Theodore Roosevelt presidency, when the entire harbor defense system was modernized. As part of that program, the long "Pull, yank and be damned" point that had caused so much difficulty in sailing up the river was dynamited into silt. The house situated on the site belonged to William Lowell Hill, who was in charge of some of the Spanish prisoners and served at the Ship Yard until his death in 1922. Hill was the recipient of the Congressional Medal of Honor.
Courtesy of the Athenaeum

Ship construction at Shattuck's Shipyard in Newington, New Hampshire, during World War I. Over two thousand workers built wooden cargo ships for transport during the conflict.
Courtesy of the University of New Hampshire Media Services

Submarine launching at the Portsmouth Naval Shipyard, during World War I. From the Sweetser Collection; courtesy of Mr. and Mrs. William Warren

Submarine construction at the Portsmouth Naval Shipyard. Courtesy of Robert A. Whitehouse

*At the conclusion of World War II in Europe in May 1945, all the German naval vessels were ordered to report to the nearest Allied port. Six submarines came into Portsmouth harbor, and four of them are pictured here. Their design differed markedly from those of the American submarines, and they were carefully studied by naval personnel. According to rumor, at least one of the subs penetrated the harbor through the underwater gates. One of those subs is on exhibit in Chicago's marine museum and is reputed to be the only submarine to have navigated the Great Lakes. It is also alleged that another German sub sank just before the armistice and is situated off the coast near Rye, where it remains to this day in about 90 feet of water.
From the Sweetser Collection: courtesy of Mr. and Mrs. William Warren*

5
MAN TO MACHINES

The economy of the seacoast region passed through a half-century of important change from 1800 to 1850. In the opening decades of the nineteenth century, the people of southeastern New Hampshire continued to rely on the traditional agriculture and shipbuilding. During the first half of the nineteenth century almost five hundred ships were built along the banks of the thirteen-mile-long river. However, huge brick buildings soon began to appear along the rivers where the masts of ships under construction had once loomed.

The seacoast managed to maintain a preeminence in the political as well as the economic sphere during the years immediately following the adoption of the Federal Constitution. Although the capital had moved from Portsmouth to Exeter and finally mid-state to Concord, the seacoast continued to exercise its power despite the absence of the influence that accrues and the glamour that is attendant upon the seat of governmental power. It took years before the interior and the frontier evolved enough to draw political power away from the original settlements on the seacoast. The dominant position maintained by the Federalist party lasted through the first two decades of the nineteenth century until the Jeffersonian Republicans emerged as a new force in New Hampshire.

The growing presence of textile mills, an accelerating phenomenon before the mid-nineteenth century, presaged profound alterations in the life of seacoast New Hampshire and indeed in the life of the entire state.

Jonathan Sawyer was brought from Massachusetts by his cousin Albert Sawyer, founder of Sawyer's Mills. Albert died in his forties, and Jonathan succeeded him as head of the mills. The Sawyers made their fortune during the Civil War manufacturing cloth for the uniforms of the Union army. Jonathan Sawyer was a respected citizen of Dover for many years.
Courtesy of
Mr. and Mrs. George Frost Sawyer

Beginning with Slater's Mill in Pawtucket, Rhode Island, changes in patterns of production spread northward into southern New Hampshire and the Merrimack Valley. Soon the daughters from the farms and the farmhands flocked to the commercial centers in search of wages.

With the election of Andrew Jackson as president, the Jeffersonian Republicans emerged with the coming of industrialization as a new force in New Hampshire. With the election of Andrew Jackson, the Jeffersonian Republicans became the Democratic party. This new party's leadership began to institute a series of reforms in New Hampshire which included the abolition of imprisonment for debt, child labor laws, separation of church and state, and internal improvements. The economic base of most of the state beyond the Piscataqua was primarily agrarian, an activity in accord with the Jeffersonian predilections of the Democratic party. The independent cultivator personified values long cherished in the canons of American belief.

The power harnessed from New England's waterways made possible the construction of the many windowed red-brick textile mills that reshaped the landscape of the old towns of Dover, Newmarket, and Exeter. Even the brick was produced in another local industry. Water-powered mills had long ground the grain and shaped the timber of New England, but the rapid growth of these great brick buildings stretching along the riverfronts of quiet towns involved a new technology in textile production. Manufacturing had economic, social, and political implications. A slow and stately rhythm of life gave way to a new staccato beat, greater competition, and increased production. Country girls who first provided the labor found themselves replaced by newly arrived immigrants from Ireland and Quebec. The ethnic base changed as the economic structure evolved in new directions.

One of the first of these new enterprises appeared as early as 1803, when Nicholas Gilman of Exeter established a woolen mill on the Exeter River. Although a second pioneering venture appeared with the construction of a small cotton mill at Pickpocket Falls, the effects of the Industrial Revolution did not become fully manifest until 1827, when entrepreneurs including Nathaniel and John Taylor Gilman and Paine Wingate incorporated the Exeter Manufacturing Company. Three years later, with one brick factory building completed, production of cotton goods began. Growth was rapid. By the year 1888, the factory was producing four million yards of cloth annually, a

Sawyer mansion in Dover, New Hampshire, which was built by Jonathan Sawyer, owner of Sawyer's Mills after the Civil War. Today the site is the home of a Burger King restaurant. This house seems like the inspiration for Booth Tarkington's The Magnificent Ambersons. *Courtesy of* Mr. and Mrs. George Frost Sawyer

figure that increased to twenty-five million by 1925.

Rapid growth resulted from a favorable economic climate; the Exeter Company had begun operations during a period of high tariff rates in the wake of the War of 1812 and at a time when commercial ventures could take advantage of available capital. Technical improvements such as the power loom increased productive capacity and labor was cheap. The first employees, mostly local women, averaged a thirteen-hour working day, and a regulation stated that they must live within five minutes' walking distance from the mill. Waves of immigrants from Europe and Canada continued to make up a large share of the work force.

Similar developments occurred almost simultaneously in Dover. Transportation was substantially improved with the 1797 erection of the Piscataqua Bridge connecting Portsmouth through Newington with Dover and then beyond to Concord. The bridge was a wooden technical marvel spanning the mouth of the Great Bay. The bridge led a precarious existence until its collapse in 1856. In the hope of further improving transportation facilities, Dover residents filed petitions in 1824 with the state legislature for the granting of a charter for construction of a canal connecting Lake Winnepesauke with Dover. Although this project did not materialize, another petition soon requested the right to run ferries "to be moved by horse-power" across the river from Dover Point to Newington. By 1831 there were six Dover-based sloops and schooners that formed a line of packets operating between Dover and Boston on a regular schedule. Three daily packets operated between Dover and Portsmouth, and shortly thereafter a steamboat puffed up the Piscataqua to Dover. Soon after that the railroad arrived in the Garrison City.

As the textile business in Dover grew, the transportation facilities also increased in proportion. On April 24, 1813, David L. Currier and Richard Gove informed the public that they would engage in a cloth dressing and coloring business at Currier's Mills and "for the accommodation of their customers, at this critical moment when MONEY appears to have *taken wings*, they will gladly receive in payment for their labor such good things as the *Earth brings* forth." By 1824, when Alfred Sawyer purchased what had formerly been Libby's Mills and founded a company that later became Sawyer's Woolen Company, the economy had presumably advanced beyond the barter stage.

View of a table setting in the Sawyer mansion. The photo also demonstrates the passion for potted palms in the "Gilded Age."
Courtesy of
Mr. and Mrs. George Frost Sawyer

Jonathan Sawyer's son, Charles, became governor of New Hampshire in 1887. At his inauguration at the State House in Concord, New Hampshire, Sawyer (second from left) was flanked by the other governors of the New England states.
Courtesy of
Mr. and Mrs. George Frost Sawyer

Four years later, in 1828, an event occurred presaging future trends when the Dover Manufacturing Company ceased operations and was taken over by the newly incorporated Cocheco Company. Resident owners gave way to Boston management, indicating loss of local autonomy that found some compensation in increased production. By the spring of 1830, the weekly packet from Dover transported more cotton and woolen goods to the Boston market than the packet *New England* brought from Liverpool. Chauvinistic pride produced the assertion that cotton goods once purchased in England for thirty-eight cents per yard and thought "remarkably cheap, were not better cottons than can be purchased here at twenty cents."

This confident mood suffered a reversal when, in 1834, the mills of the Cocheco Manufacturing Company closed owing to a "turn out of the female operatives." A reduction in pay caused this very early attempt at industrial protest. Other shutdowns followed when summer droughts brought water shortages. Not until later in the nineteenth century, when water gave way to steam, could the mills be assured of a constant power supply. Electricity replaced steam in the early twentieth century.

While textiles dominated the economic life of Exeter and Dover, the brewing of ale became the largest business in Portsmouth in the latter half of the nineteenth century. The Frank Jones Brewing Company, Ltd., was the creation of Frank Jones, "king of the alemakers," and for much of his life Portsmouth's most colorful citizen." Jones was a notable exception in an enterprise that came to be virtually monopolized by German-American brewers. In that roisterous era, the Gilded Age, the Portsmouth tycoon did not confine his endeavors to the brewing of ale. He directed his restless energy into achieving a position of prominence in the Boston and Maine Railroad, far-flung hotel and resort interests, insurance, and politics, including a stint as a

representative in Congress.

In the 1850s, an Englishman named John Swindell began an ale brewing business, and in 1858 he went into partnership with the twenty-six-year-old Northwood native Frank Jones. The next year the young entrepreneur and his brother Nathaniel Jones bought out the interest of the Englishman, and Jones Brewery began its prosperous existence. The plant expanded steadily; even the Civil War failed to impede its growth. In the midst of that conflict Jones constructed a new malt house, an imposing brick edifice which remains to this day.

Jones built the largest enterprise in Portsmouth. Soon his reach extended beyond New Hampshire; he entered into partnership and acquired a brewery in South Boston in 1875. By 1883 Jones employed about five hundred men at the Portsmouth establishment and was the country's largest brewer of ale. His ambitious son-in-law, Charles Sinclair, shared an interest in many of the enterprises that constituted the far-flung Jones empire. Jones' fascination with hotels led to his acquisition of the Hotel Wentworth in Newcastle, another hotel in Boston, and the Rockingham in Portsmouth. The Rockingham had a special place in Jones's affections. His face is carved in the brownstone facade and stares out over the city that he dominated through most of his life. It is not surprising, as Ray Brighton noted in his biography of Jones, when a small child in Portsmouth was asked who made him, he replied, "Why, Frank Jones."

The end of the nineteenth century produced other forms of manufacturing in Portsmouth, notably a shoe factory and a button factory. The navy yard continued to be a large source of employment. Shipbuilding, however, declined as did agriculture. The economic life for the area focused on the mills of Dover, Exeter and Newmarket.

Exeter Manufacturing Company mill as it was about the 1870s.
Courtesy of the Exeter Historical Society

A 1988 view of the Newmarket Mills built in 1869 by the Newmarket Manufacturing Company of traprock, an igneous rock found in steplike patterns. The mill was owned by the Gallant family.
Courtesy of Paul Farrell

Mills at Newmarket, New Hampshire, were all textile mills until the 1930s, when the Little Yankee Shoe Company transformed the operations. Now the mills are going the way of many of these old edifices, conversion to condominiums.
Photo by Paul Farrell

Stereopticon slide of the Cocheco Mills looking towards the Lower Square in Dover in the mid-nineteenth century. Courtesy of Robert A. Whitehouse

A 1988 view of the Exeter Manufacturing Company's mills. Photo by Paul Farrell

Another 1870 view of the same company's mills. Courtesy of the Exeter Historical Society

*Cocheco Mills office in Dover
about 1920.
Courtesy of Robert A. Whitehouse*

*Pacific Mills, Cocheco Department,
Dover Lower Square. This picture was
taken from either the now demolished
Belknap Church or the Old City Hall.
Courtesy of Robert A. Whitehouse*

Welcome home decorations on the Company Store of the Cocheco Mills in Dover. Old Home Week was a traditional holiday in August throughout New Hampshire after the 1890s, and the tradition lasted until the Second World War. People who had moved throughout the nation returned to their native towns. In Portsmouth the celebrations were styled the "Return of the Sons of Portsmouth." Courtesy of Robert A. Whitehouse

Cocheco Manufacturing Company after the 1907 fire in Dover. Most employees escaped by ropes except for one who died when he slipped and plunged to his death.
Courtesy of Robert A. Whitehouse

At one time Portsmouth Shoe Factory was one of the area's largest employers. Most of the communities in the seacoast were once known for the manufacture of shoes.
Courtesy of Robert A. Whitehouse

John Parker Hale, a congressman of the pre-Civil War era, was born in Rochester, New Hampshire, in 1806. He practiced law in Dover, New Hampshire, and was elected to the U.S. Congress in 1824 as a Democrat. An outspoken opponent of slavery, he broke with his party on that issue. He opposed the annexation of Texas as a slave state. A coalition of Whigs and independent Democrats in the New Hampshire Legislature elected him to the U.S. Senate in 1847. He served as chairman of the Committee on Naval Affairs during the Civil War and was responsible for the end of flogging in the navy. Less acclaimed was his abolition of the grog ration, which had allowed sailors a measure of alcohol on each trip.

Hale was accused of questionable political activities when he accepted a fee from a man convicted of fraud. He was defeated for reelection in 1864. Lincoln appointed him minister to Spain, where diplomatic service landed him in further difficulties. He had an alleged amorous relationship with the Queen of Spain. He was also accused of abusing his importation franchise.

Recalled in 1869, he spent some time traveling in Europe, returning home in broken health. He died in 1873 in Dover, New Hampshire. His home is now the Woodman Institute. In spite of his problems in public life, his opposition to slavery and his advocacy of humane policies mark his public life as one of early reform.
Courtesy of Robert A. Whitehouse

This is Maplewood Farms on Woodbury Avenue in Portsmouth and the home of Frank Jones. This view shows the similarity in the Renaissance style of Jones's home and the hotel he enlarged on Newcastle, the Wentworth.
From the collection of Bruce E. Ingmire

Train arriving at the Dover station with the Hotel Kimball in the background.
Courtesy of Robert A. Whitehouse

W. C. Brown Box Factory in Epping,
New Hampshire.
From the David Sanborn Collection;
courtesy of the Epping Historical Society

*Workers at the Granite State brickyard
in Epping, New Hampshire.
Courtesy of the Epping Historical Society
and John Lauoie*

6
LITERARY HAUNT AND PEOPLE'S RESORT

Since the eighteenth century, seacoast writers of New Hampshire have contributed to American Literature. The popularity of their works led readers to visit the region. The first such notable work appeared in 1726, when Samuel Penhallow, a Portsmouth magistrate, published *The History of the Wars of New England with the Eastern Indians*, a realistic account of the sanguinary conflicts endured by the early settlers of the area.

The following year, the Reverend Jabez Fitch, a popular Portsmouth clergyman, published a sermon in which he exhorted his congregation to repent after God's warning to them in the form of a "great" earthquake. Farmers like Samuel Lane of Stratham kept diaries that, when published posthumously, became mines of information detailing eighteenth-century rural life and creating a nostalgia about the old days on a coastal farm.

The first major literary effort detailing the history of the seacoast came from the pen of the Reverend Jeremy Belknap. While he was pastor of the Dover Congregational Church during the years of the American Revolution, he researched and wrote his acclaimed *History of New Hampshire*. Of a less serious nature, in 1800 Portsmouth native Henry Sherburne published *The Oriental Philanthropist or True Republican*, the first novel written and published in New Hampshire. The following year,. Tabitha Gilman Tenney of Exeter published her amusing *Female Quixotism: Exhibited in the Romantic Opinions and Extravagant Adventures of Dorcasina Sheldon*, a satire on popular, romantic literary modes.

These early efforts were scattered and separated by long, arid stretches when little of literary merit materialized. With the exception of Charles Brewster's engaging *Rambles About Portsmouth*, first published in 1859, little else left local presses that attracted wide attention at the time of the War Between the States. It was not until after the Civil War that the seacoast region's "golden age" began.

"I thought Rivermouth the prettiest place in the world, and I think so still," enthused Thomas Bailey Aldrich. "We who are Tiverton born," Alice Brown reminisced, "have a way of shutting our eyes now and then to present changes, and seeing things as they were once." Celia Thaxter dubbed the Isles of Shoals "enchanted islands" and remarked that the natives "find it almost as difficult to tear themselves away as do the Swiss to leave their mountains . . . . No other place is able to furnish the inhabitants of the Shoals with sufficient air for their capacious lungs; there is never enough scope elsewhere, there is no horizon; they must have sea-room."

Each of these three writers maintained an intimate connection with the New Hampshire seacoast. Aldrich's *Story of a Bad Boy* remains the quintessential American "rite of passage" novel in its evocation of happy childhood and the transition of Tom Bailey from boy to responsible young adult. Rivermouth is, of course, Portsmouth where "a beautiful river goes rippling by the town, and after turning and twisting, among a lot of tiny islands, empties itself into the sea." Similarly in his *Real Diary of a Real Boy*, Henry Shute wrote a humorous account of his early life in Exeter, Alice Brown's Tiverton is the Hampton Falls of her girlhood, peopled with colorful, frequently eccentric village folk whose lives provided inspiration for her short stories. In her poetry and essays, Celia Leighton Thaxter, a descendant of pioneer settlers to the region, displayed an ardent sense of place and a profound attachment to the Isles of Shoals.

Nearby in South Berwick, Maine, Thaxter's long-time friend, Sarah Orne Jewett in her *Country of the Pointed Firs* produced a work redolent with the atmosphere of southern Maine and the Piscataqua. Jewett, a frequent visitor in Portsmouth, also spent time with her grandfather in Exeter and came to know the area intimately when she accompanied her father, a physician, on his rounds.

Samuel Clemens came to Maine in the summer and stayed at York Harbor. His editor, William Dean Howells, was first to describe the area to Clemens when Howells chose Kittery Point for a summer residence. Howells, dean of American letters, edited the *Atlantic Monthly* in which most of these writers were published. Howells converted a barn to a library where he wrote during the last years of his life. He called the studio his "barnbrary."

The literary reputation of Portsmouth native James T. Fields, a poet of modest accomplishments, rests primarily on his work as a publisher, as a partner in the firm Ticknor and Fields, and also as an editor of the *Atlantic Monthly*. His wife, Annie, friend of Jewett and with her co-editor of the correspondence of Celia Thaxter, maintained an important literary salon on Charles Street in Boston. Artistic figures like Lowell, Whittier, Emerson, and artist Childe Hassam became acquainted through the Leighton family who operated the hotel on the Isles of Shoals.

Never had the seacoast region enjoyed such a constellation of creative talent, and each summer more literary figures were drawn to the area. Barrett Wendell took a summer home on Pleasant Street in Portsmouth which is even today called the Wendell House. Francis Parkman, the historian who dramatized New England history, wrote several chapters of his multitudinous works in his daughter's home, the former Benning Wentworth mansion on Little Harbor. Exeter was the birthplace of sculptor Daniel Chester French and Hampton that of

architect Ralph Adams Cram. Further north, Kenneth Roberts wrote novels like *Northwest Passage* with settings in the seacoast. When asked what drew all the artists and writers to the area, Roberts said that he attributed it to the iodine in the fish.

This remarkable literary period lasted throughout the latter decades of the nineteenth century and into the beginning of the twentieth. The old New England Yankee culture of the Piscataqua underwent a series of significant transitions. The Civil War, the general decline of ship-building in the Piscataqua, and the displacement of agri-culture by textile mills as the economic base of the area all combined to alter the face of its landscape.

Contemporaneously, the demographic structure of the area changed with the arrival of immigrant groups. A modern society was emerging from the older, traditional society. A number of these writers, particularly Aldrich, Brown, and Shute drew their inspiration from their native towns and from the era of their childhood. For those living in the new age, the seeming innocence of pre-Civil War days held a nostalgic charm. As they faced the challenge of a new century, it may have been comforting to look back to the old days on the seacoast and to view that time as one of romantic charm and idealized community.

Once the beauty of New Hampshire's seacoast was publicized through the works of artists, everyone wanted to experience its charms. By the mid-nineteenth century

A Star Island, Isles of Shoals, cottage about 1910. From the Sweetser Collection; courtesy of Mr. and Mrs. William Warren

the railroad brought vacationers to the burgeoning number of hotels that stood on the shoreline from Hampton Beach to Newcastle. Humble boardinghouses often gave way to grand establishments with turrets, mansard roofs and sweeping verandas. Although these opulent caravanseries attracted the more affluent clientele, smaller inns and cottages served those of more modest income who sought seaside recreation and inspiration in Hampton, Hampton Beach, Rye, and the Isles of Shoals.

As the Industrial Revolution created a higher standard of living, the middle class, whose free time had been spent at home, could now afford a holiday by the sea. With cheaper transportation available and the increasing popularity of the automobile, areas hitherto considered inaccessible came within the purview of those whose forebears had seldom departed their home counties.

The first area resort hotel rose at Hampton Beach early in the nineteenth century, followed by inns located

*The Sweetser family, like many other natives of the area, made a summer pilgrimage to Celia's Isles and recorded the event in this Kodak print.
From the Sweetser Collection; courtesy of Mr. and Mrs. William Warren*

on the winding roads of Rye. City people came to pursue the amenities of country life; while serving in the Civil War, a Union officer wrote wistfully recalling his duck-hunting holidays spent along the marshes adjacent to the shores of Rye. Out at sea was the Isles of Shoals retreat; the Leighton family built a hotel on Appledore Island. Nearby stood the cottage of Celia Leighton Thaxter, hostess to the artistic and literary greats of New England. The New Hampshire seacoast, once an attraction for

intellectuals, now entertained seekers of pleasures.

Foremost among these newer resorts were Newcastle's Wentworth-by-the-Sea and the Farragut House in Rye. The latter, operated successfully in the post-World War II years by William Cotter, was torn down in the 1970s. The Wentworth, whose future now stands in a precarious state, still survives, although it ceased operation about five years ago. As it is now, some of the building may be saved, but a substantial portion may be razed as fire

*View of the back yard at the Thomas
Bailey Aldrich House at Strawbery
Banke, Inc., where the young Tom
Bailey, hero of* The Story of A Bad
Boy *lived.
Courtesy of the University of
New Hampshire Media Services,
Gary Sampson*

*Unidentified bathers at the beach
about 1890.
Courtesy of Strawbery Banke, Inc.*

insurance standards no longer allow the building to remain as it is.

Wentworth Hall was constructed in 1873-1874. The name was changed to Hotel Wentworth in 1876, and three years later Frank Jones became the principal owner. Immediately, improvements were made and the hotel became a favorite with the wealthy. When the Treaty of Portsmouth was negotiated in 1905, diplomats of Russia and Japan made their home at the Wentworth, and discussions leading to the treaty were conducted there. After the Second World War, the stately old hotel enjoyed a renaissance under the ownership of Mr. and Mrs. James Barker Smith. Today condominiums occupy its former grounds. To commemorate the eightieth anniversary (1985) of the signing of the treaty, a Japanese television company filmed part of the documentary there. For a brief moment the hotel relived its past glory: vintage automobiles lined its driveway; actors and actresses garbed in Edwardian elegance strolled its lawns. High over its roof floated the rising sun of Japan and the Russian imperial eagle.

With the exception of those who own vacation residences, the summer-long visitor is no more. Condominiums proliferate from Hampton Beach northward. The newest hotel and condominium complex, the Sheraton Harborside, opened its doors in the spring of 1988 in Portsmouth on the site of the lands owned in the seventeenth century by the first chief executive of New Hampshire, President John Cutts. It is designed to serve year-round travelers, not just the seasonal visitor. There still remains much to attract the summer sojourner to these shores. The Prescott Park Arts Festival, Market Square Day Weekend, the Elderhostel at U.N.H., the Hampton Theater, harbor cruises, trips to the Shoals, historic homes, and the museum Strawbery Banke, Inc. augment the beaches, golf courses, and nature trails. The New Hampshire seacoast now offers both intellectual and recreational pastimes for the modern devotee of the *mens sana* in *corpore sano* mentality. Today it is still a mecca for writers and artists, although it now has a year-round reputation.

Picture of Celia's parlor with all its art work and memorabilia displayed lovingly. It was the subject of a Childe Hassam painting.
Courtesy of the University of New Hampshire Media Services

Exeter's World War I Memorial by Daniel Chester French, a native of Exeter, is situated in the park near the Exeter Inn and St. Michael's Church.
Photo by Paul Farrell

Alice Brown was born in Hampton Falls, New Hampshire, in 1856. She moved to Boston, where she was associated with the Youth's Companion, *a magazine. She achieved success with the publication of fiction emphasizing local color, based on memories of her girlhood in New Hampshire. Among here works are the collected short stories,* Meadow-Grass: Tales of New England Life *(1895) and novels which include* Jeremy Hamlin *(1934). She died in 1948 in Boston.*
Courtesy of the Boston Athenaeum

91

Henry Augustus Shute was born in Exeter, New Hampshire, in 1856. He served as a judge and for relaxation played in the town band. His novel, The Real Diary of a Real Boy, *was published in 1902 and is a fictional account of his boyhood in Exeter. Shute died in 1943. Courtesy of the University of New Hampshire Media Services*

An 1891 picture of the "boys" (members) inside the Athenaeum at 9 Market Square. The picture shows the entry room before the more recent Federal-style restoration. A corporation called the Proprietors of the Athenaeum was created by the New Hampshire Legislature in 1817. The present building was constructed by John Pierce in 1803 for the New Hampshire Fire and Marine Insurance Company, which failed during the War of 1812. The building, an elegant example of the early Federal style, became the property of the Athenaeum Corporation, a private library, in 1817. Courtesy of the Athenaeum

*Louis DeRochemont was descended from
the earliest settlers, the Walfords and the
Peverlys. His own family, however, settled
in Newington. He became a noted film
producer. Among the acclaimed motion
pictures that he produced were* Martin
Luther, Windjammer, Walk East on
Beacon, The House on Ninety-Second
Street, Cinerama Holiday, *and* The
Roman Spring of Mrs. Stone. *Always
interested in important issues, he produced* Whistle at Eaton Falls, *which dealt
with technological unemployment, and*
Lost Boundries, *which confronted problems of race relations. The former was
filmed in Exeter and the latter in and
about Portsmouth. A master of the documentary film, he was the producer of*
The March of Time *series. He received
two Academy awards for his work.
Among his other honors was the
Norwegian Order of St. Olaf.
Courtesy of Mrs. Louis DeRochemont*

The Bluebird *and the lure of sailing on Great Bay with Myles Standish Watson at the age of fourteen.*
Courtesy of Dorothy Watson

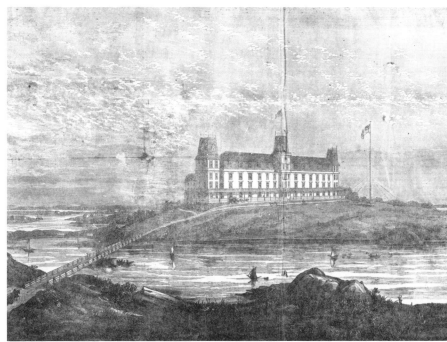

Sketch of the early Wentworth Hotel in Newcastle, which officially opened on June 20, 1874.
Courtesy of Mr. and Mrs. James Barker Smith

Postcard view of Newcastle's Wentworth Hotel showing the original boat facilities. In 1879 Frank Jones and a Mr. Beckwith remodeled the hotel and added a story, the towers, and the "Swiss chalet" roof, which was the hotel's description of its mansard roof.
Courtesy of Mr. and Mrs. James Barker Smith

Frederick Childe Hassam is posing with two friends on the great rocks on the Shoals coastline. He was a noted American artist born in Dorchester, Massachusetts, in 1859. He attended Boston Art School, studied in Paris, and came under the influence of Monet. He was a member of the "Ten," a group of impressionist painters formed in the year 1898. Friendship with Celia Thaxter brought him to the Isles of Shoals and during one visit he painted an interior scene of the Thaxter cottage that is one of his best paintings. His watercolors of her beautiful flower garden served as illustrations in her book of poetry. Hassam died in East Hampton, New York, in 1935.
Courtesy of the University of
New Hampshire Media Services

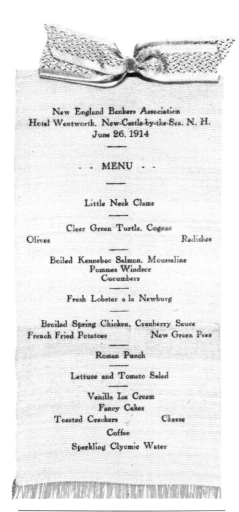

New England Bankers Association
Hotel Wentworth, New-Castle-by-the-Sea, N. H.
June 26, 1914

—

· · MENU · ·

—

Little Neck Clams

—

Clear Green Turtle, Cognac
Olives   Radishes

—

Boiled Kennebec Salmon, Mousseline
Pommes Windsor
Cucumbers

—

Fresh Lobster a la Newburg

—

Broiled Spring Chicken, Cranberry Sauce
French Fried Potatoes   New Green Peas

—

Roman Punch

—

Lettuce and Tomato Salad

—

Vanilla Ice Cream
Fancy Cakes
Toasted Crackers   Cheese

Coffee
Sparkling Clyomic Water

A menu from the Wentworth Hotel just before World War I. During that war the "gingerbread" decoration was removed.
Courtesy of Mr. and Mrs. James Barker Smith

View of Wentworth in the 1950s, when the Smiths continued to add to the reputation of the resort.
Courtesy of Mr. and Mrs. James Barker Smith

An 1888 advertisement for a tennis tournament at the Wentworth Hotel. That year another story was added to the structure. New management also constructed a dining room wing. Another operation was commenced in the "Colonial wing" that year. The Colonial wing was joined to the main hotel later.
Courtesy of Mr. and Mrs. James Barker Smith

WRIGHT & D. TSON'S
SEVENTH ANNUAL
LAWN TENNIS TOURNAMENT,
JULY 31, 1888.

This house on Red Mill Lane in Rye was the Charles Austin Jeness House built prior to the Civil War. After that war it served as a boardinghouse.
Courtesy of the Rye Historical Society

The 1885 site of the Sea View Hotel in Rye Beach is now the lcoation of the Rye, New Hampsire, United States Post Office.
Courtesy of the Rye Historical Society

The Old Admiral Farragut House in Rye before the turn of the century. It was last owned by William Cotter and was demolished in 1975.
Courtesy of the Rye Historical Society

The Farragut House in 1950 as seen from the ocean.
Courtesy of Mrs. Patricia Cotter

The Farragut Hotel Pool - Rye Beach, N.H.

The Farragut House and the pool as it was about 1950.
Courtesy of Mrs. Patricia Cotter

Portsmouth's Rockingham Hotel was decked out in 1884, just before the fire of 1884. The owner, Portsmouth's colorful brewer Frank Jones, ordered the hotel rebuilt, and his resurrected hotel stands to this date in 1989. No longer a hotel, it survives as condominiums. For many years it has been the favorite dining place for area residents. Notable among proprietors were Mr. and Mrs. James Barker Smith. Many famous Americans, including several presidents, have been guests at the hotel. The bunting in the photograph is honoring Lt. Adolphus Greeley, an arctic explorer.
Courtesy of Mr. and Mrs. James Barker Smith

This print of about 1830 shows one of the seacoast's earliest hotels, the Atlantic House, Rye Beach, New Hampshire. Courtesy of the Rye Historical Society

The interior of the Rye Beach Club. Courtesy of the Rye Historical Society

The American House, Dover, New Hampshire, as it appeared about 1890. It was torn down in the 1950s. Courtesy of Robert A. Whitehouse

99

A photograph from about 1890 of the Ocean Wave Hotel on Ocean Boulevard in Rye.
Courtesy of the Rye Historical Society

This is one of the Fuller houses along Ocean Boulevard and is typical of the large, handsome homes that grace the New Hampshire coastline.
Courtesy of the Rye Historical Society

An early view of the seacoast looking north from Rye.
Courtesy of the Rye Historical Society

This floating dock was part of the operation of the Appledore Hotel at the Isles of Shoals. The dock was devised as a unique and efficient way to expedite the disembarkation of passengers arriving on the ferry from Portsmouth
From the Sweetser Collection; courtesy of Mr. and Mrs. William Warren

This area of Ocean Boulevard was known as Locke's Neck until Governor Straw lived on the site and his name came to be applied to that area of land. About 1984 the town of Rye restored the historic name to the site, known once again as Locke's Neck.
Courtesy of the Rye Historical Society

The floating dock.
From the Sweetser Collection; courtesy of Mr. and Mrs. William Warren

*Another view of the floating dock.
From the Sweetser Collection; courtesy of
Mr. and Mrs. William Warren*

*Hampton Beach and Casino with its
Opera House about 1910 looking north.
The Bijou theater was showing movies
by then.
From the Sweetser Collection; courtesy of
Mr. and Mrs. William Warren*

*Hampton Beach when theater was
doing better than opera, about 1920.
From the Sweetser Collection; courtesy of
Mr. and Mrs. William Warren*

Hampton Beach just north of the Casino area, about 1915. One can also discern the columns of the Ashworth Hotel.
From the Sweetser Collection; courtesy of Mr. and Mrs. William Warren

This postcard view near the bandstand at Hampton Beach shows the arrival of the trolley. In the background is Great Boar's Head to the northeast.
From the Sweetser Collection; courtesy of Mr. and Mrs. William Warren

From High Street in Hampton, New Hampshire, about 1890, one would cross Lafayette Road to the railroad water tower.
From the Sweetser Collection; courtesy of Mr. and Mrs. William Warren

The Whittier Inn in Hampton, New
Hampshire, about 1880 was on the site
of 1989's Odessey House.
From the Sweetser Collection; courtesy of
Mr. and Mrs. William Warren

A closer photograph of the water tower
(far right) in Hampton, New Hampshire.
From the Sweetser Collection; courtesy of
Mr. and Mrs. William Warren

This is a 1900 picture of the Hampton
Fire Department delivering fire extin-
guishers throughout the town.
From the Sweetser Collection; courtesy of
Mr. and Mrs. William Warren

Hampton, New Hampshire, about 1910.
This is a northerly view of the busy
corner of Lafayette Road and High
Street. Two forms of transportation
dominate: the horse and buggy and the
trolley from Exeter to Hampton. The
trolley system provided an efficient mass
transit network at the time.
From the Sweetser Collection; courtesy of
Mr. and Mrs. William Warren

Portsmouth Yacht Club, which used to be situated where the foot of the Prescott Memorial Bridge is located in 1989. Curiously, the Portsmouth Yacht Club is now located in the town of Newcastle, as is the Kittery Point Yacht Club. Since the Portsmouth Naval Shipyard is located in Kittery, Maine, there is a long tradition of maritime "misnomers."
From the collection of Bruce E. Ingmire

Trolley car of the Portsmouth Electric Railroad at Lang's Corner, Rye, New Hampshire, about 1900.
Courtesy of Strawbery Banke, Inc.

Here is an 1880 photograph of what appears to be six teams of horses drawing snow-rolling equipment past the corner of Lafayette and Winnicunnet roads. In those days the snow was rolled to allow sleighs to course the roads. The photographer is looking east at the corner where the Whittier Inn was located (to the left of the picture).
From the Sweetser Collection; courtesy of Mr. and Mrs. William Warren

*Exeter Street Railway Company in
Exeter. The building to the left in the
picture still exists.
Courtesy of Strawbery Banke, Inc.*

Originally the Broadhead Methodist Episcopal Church, this building was erected when the State Street Methodists split. The dedication of the church was held April 30, 1860. In November of that same year, the Methodists reunited and the church was sold to the Baptists. It remains the Central Baptist Annex in 1989.
Courtesy of the Athenaeum

7
FAMILY LIFE IN PHOTOGRAPHS

The eighteenth-century Dover Quaker Meeting House, where poet John Greenleaf Whittier's parents were married.
Courtesy of Robert C. Whitehouse

This is North Hampton, New Hampshire, showing the community church as early as 1860. Today this is the corner of Route 101 C and Post Road. The schoolhouse was located next door.
From the Sweetser Collection; courtesy of Mr. and Mrs. William Warren

This is a view of the same location, but the church has had a second story added and the school has been rebuilt.
From the Sweetser Collection; courtesy of Mr. and Mrs. William Warren

Recent photo of the Newington Church showing the addition of landscaping. Courtesy of the Langdon Library, Newington, New Hampshire

Newington Church about 1900. Courtesy of the Langdon Library, Newington, New Hampshire

A stereoscopic photo of Dover's St. Thomas Episcopal Church. This building was replaced by the present structure on Hale Street, and the City Hall is situated where the church had been. Courtesy of Robert C. Whitehouse

The Episcopal Christ Church of Portsmouth was situated on Madison Street. Mrs. G. H. Marsh left money for the construction of the church, which allowed for free seating. It was dedicated on July 3, 1883. On June 19, 1963, it was destroyed by fire, while the fire chiefs were meeting at the Wentworth Hotel. Even though they rushed to the scene, all the fire chiefs and all the firemen couldn't put out the blaze. Today the Madison Street Apartments are located on the site.
Courtesy of the Athenaeum

A postcard view of Portsmouth's Market Square aobut 1925. This shows the Glebe Building in back of the North Church and the Hunking Wentworth House, which is across Church Street and is without the Eagle Photo aluminum facade of the mid-twentieth century. In the 1690s a stockade was built along the route of Pleasant Street, and each end was secured by a fort. One fort was approximately on the site of today's North Church. The fortification served to protect Portsmouth from Indian attack during King William's War.

In 1758 Royal Governor Wentworth elected to build a State House in the throat of King Street (Congress Street in 1989). The North Church faced east. The arrangement of the new state house created a quadrangle facing down 1989's Pleasant Street. The inhabitants then called it The Parade, and the town's militia was reported to fall in at the site. In the 1760s this area's upgrading was instigated by printer Daniel Fowle in his New Hampshire Gazette. By then his

second house of publication was located on the corner where the Athenaeum is in 1989. He moved from Pleasant Street after his wife's death in 1762. With the printer's assistance, buisnessmen held a lottery to pave what we call Market Street and make it a business center.

After the Revolution, the State House became the courthouse and was used for that purpose until 1837.
From the collection of Bruce E. Ingmire

Portsmouth's Immaculate Conception Roman Catholic Church on Summer Street was nineteenth-century gothic architecture. Completed in 1873, it replaced an earlier wooden church which burned in 1871. Parts of this church were saved in 1933, when the present church was built.
Courtesy of the Athenaeum

An outdoor picture of Portsmouth's Universalist Sunday School class in the late 1920s. Some of the participants in the first row include William Smart, Garland Ferry, Bernard Hollings, and Robert Miller. In the second row, among the students, are Kenneth Drew, Wallace Garrett, Robert Ferry, Phil Smart, B. Drew, and Fred Hand. In the last row are Muriel Clark, Wallace and Francis Clark Chatterton, Mable Shedd, and one of the Redden sisters.
Courtesy of the Smart family

*A gathering of locals of Portsmouth's
St. John's Episcopal Church Parish House
formerly located on State Street next to
the Mathew Marsh House. It was one of
the few Greek Revival buildings and is
now gone.
Courtesy of Strawbery Banke, Inc.*

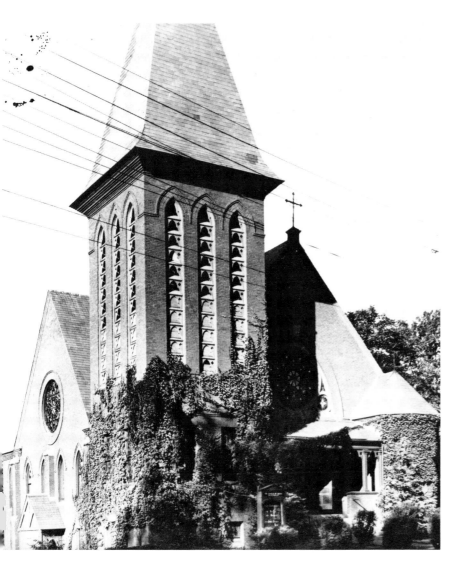

The brick Universalist Church on Pleasant Street in Portsmouth was built in 1896 after the wooden church was burned.
Courtesy of Unitarian Universalist Church

The Unitarian Church on State Street in Portsmouth, the only Greek Revival public building that remains in Portsmouth, is also the South Church. It marks the home of a congregation that not only was preeminent in the Unitarian movement but that has remained a consistent voice of toleration. The building, constructed by Jonathan Folsom in 1826, shows an ivy covering as it looked in 1920. The look is nostalgic but no longer advisable.
Courtesy of Unitarian Universalist Church

The interior of the South Church showing the classical decoration that remains as of 1989. Note the vaulted ceiling and the engaged Corinthian columns. After the 1947 fire destroyed the Universalist Church on Pleasant Street, the remaining communicants united with the Unitarians, presaging a nationwide union in 1960 creating the Unitarian Universalist Church.
Courtesy of Unitarian Universalist Church

Portsmouth's South Meetinghouse became the Children's Museum of Portsmouth in 1983.
Courtesy of Strawbery Banke, Inc.

The Middle Street Baptist Church showing the corps of cadets. Courtesy of the Athenaeum

The Wedgewood School in Rye Center about 1907. The school was later destroyed by fire. The twin girls (center) dressed in the matching middy blouses are Hilda and Hazel Berry. The girl to the extreme left with the white hair bow is Doris Berry Keene. The girl with the white skirt seated in front of the third boy from the left in the back row is Lizzie Caswell.
Courtesy of the Rye Historical Society

East School in Rye, New Hampshire, was resplendent for Christmas 1903 when this photograph was taken. There is a Christmas verse on the blackboard. Note the piano in the right foreground and the box stove in the center of the photograph.
Courtesy of the Rye Historical Society

Known as the Goodwin Perkins House on Perkins Road, Rye, this late 1800s Eastlake stick house was built by James Henry Perkins. It burned after World War II, but its barn and outbuildings survive to this day.
Courtesy of the Rye Historical Society

Green Gables, possibly designed by William Hunt Morris, showing the construction crew on the site. It is located near today's Abanaki Golf Course and is not visible from the road. Built by a man named Dibble from Chicago, Illinois, the house was later purchased by Richard Morton for his family. Morton owned a large amount of real estate in Portsmouth during the 1960s.
Courtesy of the Rye Historical Society

This is an 1886 photograph of a few of the young British employees of the cable station. The Rye Cable Station was built in the mid-nineteenth century and was the first terminus of the Atlantic cable in North America. The men had caught the baseball enthusiasm.
Courtesy of the Rye Historical Society

This is an interior picture of Samuel Allen's parlor in the house on the corner of Sea and Central roads in Rye, New Hampshire.
Courtesy of the Rye Historical Society

A photograph dating from 1890 and showing a wedding at the Rye Christian Church which burned and was replaced by the Brown Church. The Brown Church was later dismantled.
Courtesy of the Rye Historical Society

House on Red Mill Lane, Rye, New Hampshire, built by Jacob Marston, architect and contractor, on land given by Samuel Jenness. Jenness's son Otis Simpson Jenness married Marston's daughter, Anne Parsons Marston. The house was a wedding gift.
Courtesy of the Rye Historical Society

Rye resident John Foss.
Courtesy of the Rye Historical Society

One of a series of pictures of Rye, New Hampshire, by Alba R. H. Foss, a local and prominent photographer. Foss married Minnie Brown and then Emma Hoyt and died in 1935. His family owned this, the Foss Boarding House.

Bertha Foss is in the center. This building, located on Washington Road, burned. The picture includes other, unidentified members of the Foss family.
Courtesy of the Rye Historical Society

This A. R. H. Foss portrait captures a popular image of the Victorian protectors of morality who peopled New England villages like Rye or Newington. Courtesy of the Rye Historical Society

Hannah Pollard in a photograph taken by A. R. H. Foss. Courtesy of the Rye Historical Society

The young Florence Coleman (Mrs. Myles Standish Watson). Courtesy of the Langdon Library, Newington, New Hampshire

Class of 1905, Portsmouth High School.
Florence Coleman is the young lady on
the right.
Courtesy of Dorothy Watson

Portrait of Isaac Dow, a prosperous
farmer of the late nineteenth century
who was descended from early settlers.
Courtesy of the Langdon Library,
Newington, New Hampshire

Isaac Dow posed at his Newington home,
which in 1989 is near a highway junction and the site of a popular restaurant.

Courtesy of the Langdon Library,
Newington, New Hampshire

A formal portrait with James Cowan Sawyer, Mary Pepperrell Frost (Mrs. J. C. Sawyer), Ethel Devin, and Jeremiah Smith, Jr.
Courtesy of Mr. and Mrs. George Frost Sawyer

Lawn tennis and 19 "ought" fashions with the Sawyer family. James Cowan Sawyer is in the front (right) with two others who remain unidentified. In the back row, from left to right, are Mary Pepperrell Frost, Jeremiah Smith, Jr., and Ethel Devin.
Courtesy of Mr. and Mrs. George Frost Sawyer

The Sawyers and Frosts enjoying an after-noon on the Oyster River in Durham. Courtesy of Mr. and Mrs. George Frost Sawyer

The Dover Cooking Club, 1890. Courtesy of Mr. and Mrs. George Frost Sawyer

Sailing with the Whitehouse family on Great Bay. Courtesy of Mr. Robert A. Whitehouse

Lest we forget that all life is not simply pleasure, a photograph of the office of dentist Dr. Pickering. The thought of suffering through such an operation is enough to rid anyone of the idle thought, "Oh, I wish I had lived back then...."
Courtesy of Strawbery Banke, Inc.

A Newington class, photographed about 1885.
Courtesy of the Langdon Library, Newington, New Hampshire

The DeRochemonts about 1890 on the piazza of their Newington home, now the Great Bay Training Center. The two people at the far left and the two men seated among the women are unidentified. From left to right are Henriette DeRochemont, Marie Dillingham DeRochemont, Sarah Hill DeRochemont, Emily Mitton DeRochemont, Ruth DeRochemont, Emily A. Nutter DeRochemont, and Florence Estelle DeRochemont.
Courtesy of the DeRochemont family

127

North Mill Bridge in Portsmouth about
1880, when it was Elm Street.
Courtesy of the Athenaeum

The corner at Portsmouth's Maplewood
and Dennett streets with the Franklin
School and its cupola in the background.
Before the highway intruded into the
neighborhood, the Cutts mansion stood
in the midst of a bucolic scene in this
section of Portsmouth. Originally the
Cutts dominated the section to Pulpit
Rock, and the cove, now filled in, was
called Cutts Cove. Ursula Cutts died in
an Indian raid on the site.
Courtesy of the Athenaeum

Education at the Cabot Street School
and the class of 1908. This school was
built by Benjamin Webster.
Courtesy of the Athenaeum

The late nineteenth century produced wealth in such families as that of Benjamin Webster, first a carpenter and then builder of the Kearsarge House and Cabot School. His home on Broad Street was built on Rundlett's Mountain. Today it is the Wood J. Verne Funeral Home. This combination of Italianate and Renaissance Revival styles is often called Victorian. The style is equal to the earlier Georgian Warner House or the Federal Langdon House.
Courtesy of the Athenaeum

Gilbert and Sullivan comes to Durham. There does not appear to be a woman in the cast. The explanation of the all-male ensemble has not been left to posterity, but the authors gladly await any information readers can share to shed light on the subject.
Courtesy of Dorothy Watson

This photo of the Eldridge Estate with central Portsmouth in the background was taken most likely from the top of the Webster House about 1890. The absence of trees is surprising until the reader realizes that nineteenth-century Portsmouth expanded into former farmland and onto landfill.
Courtesy of the Athenaeum

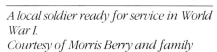

A local soldier ready for service in World War I.
Courtesy of Morris Berry and family

More formal photos of the Berrys about 1910.
Courtesy of Morris Berry and family

A formal Kodak photograph.
Courtesy of Morris Berry and family

Picture of a man beside a light at the trolley station at Newington in the beginning of the century.
Courtesy of Morris Berry and family

A typical family situated in one of the homes that is today part of the gentri-fication of Portsmouth.
Courtesy of Morris Berry and family

Nineteen eighty-eight marked the cen-tennial of the first Kodak, and many of the pictures used in this work were the result of the cameras George Eastman marketed throughout the world.
Courtesy of Morris Berry and family

The automobile comes to Portsmouth.
Courtesy of Morris Berry and family

These are early telephone operators working out of the New England Telephone offices on High Street. In 1989 that same building is Lukas, Another Restaurant.
Courtesy of Morris Berry and family

Most homes in Portsmouth at the turn of the century had outdoor "necessaries."
Courtesy of Morris Berry and family

Children on Fleet Street in Portsmouth. Notice the sign in the window indicating that the lady of the house will require a stop by the ice man.
Courtesy of Morris Berry and family

Children in a yard on Fleet Street.
Courtesy of Morris Berry and family

Unique individuals creating break-
throughs of another kind.
Courtesy of Morris Berry and family

An eccentric photographed about 1910.
Note that Marlene Dietrich in 1930 was
breaking no style barriers as far as this
woman was concerned.
Courtesy of Morris Berry and family

Fleet Street and some of the children who once frequented the area. They kept their ponies and carts in the nearby stables and were part of the charm that once was the North End of Portsmouth. Courtesy of Morris Berry and family

This is Portsmouth's Ladies Club about 1930. From left to right are Edith Wiggin, Emma Mack, Biona Smart, Dora Smart, and Freda Crowley. Courtesy of the Smart family

This is Nicky the Cat and the whole Smart family. This photo was taken at the old Assembly Building. Courtesy of the Smart family

134

Gay Earl Smart's three children—Philip, Dorothy, and William. The photo was taken in 1927 at either 144 Vaughan Street or 5 Raits Court.
Courtesy of the Smart family

Gay Earl Smart and his family at 144 Vaughan Street in Portsmouth about 1933. This is the northern half of the old Assembly Building. The house on the left rear was on the north side of Deer Street.
    The Smarts are descended from Capt. Richard Smart, who commanded the Nancy, *an early privateer. Captain Smart captured the* Resolution, *the first such prize to be brought into Portsmouth Harbor. His descendents have married into many of the families that have made Portsmouth's history and who remain dedicated to preserving that history both in museums and in written works like this.*
Courtesy of the Smart family

*Fashionably attired arrivals at the
Newington trolley station.
Courtesy of Morris Berry and family*

*A young secoast man and his girlfriend.
She appears to be concerned about the
late trolley from Portsmouth.
Courtesy of Morris Berry and family*

*A "Gibson Girl" about to take a ride on
the Great Bay.
Courtesy of Morris Berry and family*

Locals posing at the Newington trolley station.
Courtesy of Morris Berry and family

The gentleman of Goat Island was some-times referred to as "the Hermit." His name was Jim Murtaugh, and the pic-ture dates from about 1920.
Courtesy of the Newington Historical Society

The Teddy Two, *a boat owned by Dr. Whitehouse of Dover, New Hampshire, was christened twice, once on the stern and once on the bow.*
Courtesy of Robert A. Whitehouse

A view about 1890 from Portsmouth's old courthouse. The Unitarian Church is on the right. This photo, looking toward State Street, shows the nature of the city, *with the elms and the turn-of-the-century homes. Note all the gauges on the brass steam engine.*
Courtesy of Strawbery Banke, Inc.

A procession pasing by the old Rocking-ham Court House in 1897. Even at that late date the ox and horse were still an evident form of transportation. Courtesy of Strawbery Banke, Inc.

Vaughan Street was named for the Vaughan family, who married into the Cutts oligarchy. The original North End citizens of the town were firmly attached to the Puritan church and republican policies of the Massachusetts Puritan leaders. This photo shows a parade about 1890. Courtesy of Stawbery Banke, Inc.

A Portsmouth High School's football team playing on the South Playground about 1908. Courtesy of the Smart family

A Memorial Day parade in Portsmouth which featured the riding abilities of these two young men. The date is about 1915, and the picture was taken in front of the old post office on Pleasant Street. Courtesy of Morris Berry and family

Old Home Week in Dover Lower Square, 1912. Seen is the Old Town Hall Clock Tower at left, the Belknap Church (center), which is now a parking lot, and the Masonic Temple Building at the right. Courtesy of Robert A. Whitehouse

Johnny Grimes Market in Dover in the early twentieth century. Courtesy of Robert A. Whitehouse

The bandstand and monkey cage in Central Park in Somersworth, New Hampshire. The park, designed with a lake, was located on the road between Dover and Rochester. This park, on the trolley line from Dover, was favored by many of the Cocheco millworkers and their families. Like Pine Island in Manchester, this park suffered with the advent of the automobile, which permitted families to seek recreation further afield. The location has now reverted to a wild state.
Courtesy of Robert A. Whitehouse

The interior of the Opera House in Somersworth, New Hampshire, was typical of a style to be found throughout the United States when many small communities boasted an opera house.
Courtesy of Robert A. Whitehouse

Dover trolleymen James Walker and Forrest Eastman.
Courtesy of Robert A. Whitehouse

*Franklin Square with Lathrop-Farnham's
semi-annual clearance sale in Dover,
New Hampshire.
Courtesy of Robert A. Whitehouse*

*The old Durham Town Library in 1908
is private housing today. The Dimond
Library at the University of New Hamp-
shire now serves as Durham's library.
Courtesy of Mr. and Mrs. George
Frost Sawyer*

A train accident, May 3, 1909. Note the percentage of men in the picture wearing hats. The McDonough Street area is in the background.
Courtesy of Strawbery Banke, Inc.

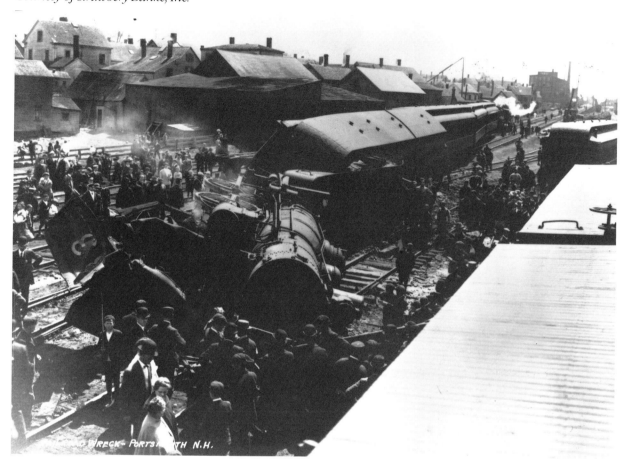

This picture presumably is the great blizzard of 1888. Needless to say, the snow buried landmarks that could have been used to identify the site. It is likely to be Coffins Court off Cabot Street. Snow after that storm of March was supposed to have stayed on the ground until June.
From the Sweetser Collection; courtesy of Mr. and Mrs. William Warren

Another stereopticon slide of winter. This photo appears to be State Street. The Mathew Marsh House is on the viewer's right. The Methodist Church was purchased in 1902 by the Jewish community and transformed into the Temple Israel. The church retains its cupola in this picture.
From a stereoscopic slide; courtesy of the Athenaeum

143

This is Congress Street in Portsmouth in the aftermath of the kind of snowstorm every New Englander loves because it usually provides excuses to avoid a day at work. The City Hotel was situated on the site of today's Odd Fellows Hall.

Across Fleet Street is the Dean House, and in the background is the cupola of the Temple, the precursor to the Music Hall.
From a Davis stereoscopic slide; courtesy of the Athenaeum

Middle Street taken after the great ice storm of 1886.
Courtesy of Strawbery Banke, Inc.

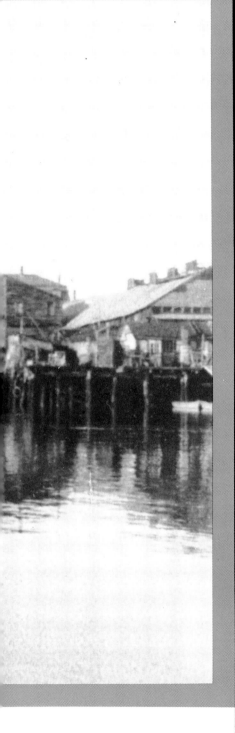

8

PORTSMOUTH IN THE NINETEENTH AND EARLY TWENTIETH CENTURY: PUBLIC BUILDINGS, WATERFRONT, AND DOWNTOWN

This Greek Revival building was erected in 1836 on the site where the 1989 Portsmouth fire station is located on Court Street. This building served as the County Court House and gave Court Street its name. After 1891 the Old Court House served as the Veterans' Memorial Hall, In 1918, when the present fire station was built, the Veterans' Memorial Hall was removed to the anterior part of the site near 1988's Parrot Avenue. Greek Revival had its popularity in the 1820s and 1830s, when the New Hampshire seacoast did not have a flourishing economy. Thus few buildings of this style were erected in the city. This example is Doric from the style of columns used in the construction.
Courtesy of the Athenaeum

The 1891 Rockingham County Court House was Romanesque in style and was located on State Street where the Piscataqua Bank drive-up window and parking lot are now located. The building burned and a new location was chosen in Exeter.
From the collection of Bruce E. Ingmire

Rockingham County Jail
Portsmouth, N. H.

In 1988 this building was still the Portsmouth Police Station on Pennhallow Street just in back of the site of the 1891 Rockingham Court House. To be sold by the city, the station will be relocated in the City Hall complex, formerly the non-profit hospital on Junkins Avenue. With all the awnings and ivy in this photo, people might have tried for a cell in the place.
From the collection of Bruce E. Ingmire

A postcard showing the 1850s United States Post Office in Portsmouth, New Hampshire. The elm trees of that era have disappeared as a result of Dutch Elm disease. The Renaissance-style building is constructed of indigenous New Hampshire granite from quarries in Raymond and Concord.
From the collection of Bruce E. Ingmire

Earliest Court Street in Portsmouth, which is today upper Pleasant Street, showing the original corner bow front of an 1989s restaurant, the Rusty Hammer. Note how the horse and buggy are attached to the posts and beams that delineate the sidewalk from the roadway. Apparently these configurations also served as anchors for awnings for first-floor commercial outlets. The streets are lined with elms, protected from the horses and buggies by wooden shields.
From the Sweetser Collection; courtesy of Mr. and Mrs. William Warren

The non-profit, early-twentieth-century Portsmouth hospital on Junkins Avenue in an early postcard view. It became the City Hall in 1988.
From the collection of Bruce E. Ingmire

149

The 1858 United States Post Office and Court House was designed by Ammi Burnham Young and built before the Civil War. Previous to its erection, the Rockingham Bank and a hotel, the Piscataqua House, were situated on the site. On the right side of the photograph is the wooden structure called the Glebe Land Building, which was destroyed by fire. Young, a New Hampshire native, also designed the Boston Customs House while he worked for the U.S. Government. The Vermont State Capitol is his design as well. Stone as a building material became more popular as the nineteenth century progressed and technology made quarrying and transportation more economical.
Courtesy of the Athenaeum

The waterfront looking toward the Naval Shipyard about 1925 after completion of the Memorial Bridge. The foreground shows an old gundalow. The rotting piers and the lack of ships demonstrate the decline in maritime activity in that era. There are coal storage units visible in the background.
Courtesy of the Athenaeum

A photo of Water Street taken just beside the Liberty Pole. These "liberty poles" have a tradition that harks to the Maypoles of "merry old England." They were erected in many American communities at the time of the American Revolution. In Boston the tradition was a liberty tree instead.
Courtesy of the Athenaeum

Street with the auxiliary power station in the background. Photo taken about 1935.
Courtesy of the Athenaeum

The infamous houses of "suspended integrity" energized the Prescott sisters into the work of social reform through the process which might be called "neighborhood redefinition." The Gloucester House is in the foreground. In 1912 the navy threatened to transfer "liberty parties" to Boston as a result of several murders on Water Street. Local merchants cooperated in a pre-World War I reestablishment of the integrity of the "homes." Prohibition, the greatest American failure, only added to the colorful history of this area, where assignations and dalliances continued to be the order of the day.
Courtesy of the Athenaeum

This photo of Water Street was taken from the opposite end, at the foot of the Memorial Bridge.
Courtesy of the Athenaeum

151

These buildings sat opposite today's
Lower Prescott Park. Once known as
Water Street because it was on the
water, the landfill allowed the citizenry
to rename the street after Daniel Marcy.
Courtesy of the Athenaeum

The Captain Shaw House was moved to
the site where the Gloucester House once
was situated, and is now the home of
Donald Margeson.
From the collection of Bruce E. Ingmire

The Captain Shaw House at its original
site on Marcy Street.
Courtesy of the Athenaeum

The junction of Newton and Water streets at the Liberty Pole. This section of town was thickly settled in the 1680s. In 1680 the street that was called Newton Street in the 1930s was water-connected to the South Mill Pond and all of it was called the Salt Marsh. At some point a stockade was erected, and the outlet to the waterway through 1988's Strawbery Banke, Inc., was named Puddle Dock after a London wharf area on the Thames. By the twentieth century the waterway had become fetid because the fresh water source out into Miller Avenue had been cut off. As a result, the bridge was erected to facilitate the passage down Water Street. This was called Swing Bridge because of the particular construction and Liberty Bridge later because of the proximity to the Liberty Pole.
Courtesy of the Athenaeum

The Liberty Pole on Marcy Street, where the swing bridge once was positioned over Puddle Dock. The Liberty Pole was erected at the time of the protest in Portsmouth over the Stamp act just before it went into effect, November 1, 1765.
Courtesy of the Athenaeum

Newton Avenue showing the junkyards and auto service businesses that marked the Depression era and would later be developed into a museum, Strawbery Banke, Inc.
Courtesy of the Athenaeum

The future Prescott Park.
Courtesy of the Athenaeum

Charles William Prescott was born in Somersworth, New Hampshire, in 1853, the son of Charles S. and Joanna Fitts Prescott. He graduated from Portsmouth Boys High School in 1869. He moved to Boston where he was employed by Jordan and Marsh. When he was twenty-four years old, in 1877, he moved to Erie, Pennsylvania, and there he and William Trask founded Trask and Prescott, which started as a dry goods store and grew into a large department store. Later Prescott invested in Lovell Manufacturing Company.

Prescott died in 1932, leaving a fortune of almost three million dollars. His surviving sisters contested the will and with their lawyer, Charles Dale, won the case and the money was given to the two schoolteachers.
Courtesy of the Athenaeum

Mary Elizabeth Prescott was born in 1855 and died in 1939. She was graduated from Portsmouth Girls' High School in 1873 and was the salutatorian of her class. From 1874 until 1890, she taught at the Haven School in Portsmouth. Later she taught at the Peabody School in Boston. Upon returning to Portsmouth, she taught at the Whipple School. After she inherited her brother's fortune, she and her sister devoted their lives to establishing Prescott Park.
Courtesy of the Athenaeum

Josephine Fitts Prescott was born in 1858 and died in 1949. She was a graduate of Portsmouth Girls' high school and served as secretary of the New Hampshire Teachers Association. Later she was employed as a clerk by the Children's Aid Society of Boston. Returning to Portsmouth, she spent the remainder of her life in her family home on Middle Street. After receiving the inheritance from her brother's estate, she worked with her sister to beautify the Marcy Street area and create Prescott Park. The park was named in honor of their father.
Courtesy of the Athenaeum

This railroad bridge to Kittery was built about 1842 next to the Portsmouth Bridge, which crossed Noble's Island and then crossed the main river to Kittery.
Courtesy of the Athenaeum

The railroad bridge to Kittery, like so many bridges of the era, was built of both wood and metal. At the end of the nineteenth century, technologists proposed that all-metal bridges were structurally more sound.
Courtesy of the Athenaeum

Portsmouth's Memorial Bridge was moved into place in 1923. It was dedicated to those who died in World War I.
From the Sweetser Collection; courtesy of Mr. and Mrs. William Warren

Memorial Bridge across the Piscataqua from Portsmouth, New Hampshire, to Kittery, Maine, was a product of the new popularity of the automobile and marked the beginning of the end of regular, local transportation across the river by boat.
From the Sweetser Collection; courtesy of Mr. and Mrs. William Warren

First contracts for the Memorial Bridge were let November 1920 for the foundation work. It was completed on March 1, 1922.
From the Sweetser Collection; courtesy of Mr. and Mrs. William Warren

Memorial Bridge's last span was set in its place on December 20, 1922.
From the Sweetser Collection; courtesy of Mr. and Mrs. William Warren

The piers for the spans of the Memorial Bridge went as much as eighty-two feet into the bedrock.
From the Sweetser Collection; courtesy of Mr. and Mrs. William Warren

The spans for the Memorial Bridge were prefabricated at Union Wharf, situated in the vicinity of the abutments of the new bridge on the Portsmouth side of the river. They were floated into position at high tide on barges.
From the Sweetser Collection; courtesy of Mr. and Mrs. William Warren

The Memorial Bridge was built by the American Bridge Company and has a Waddell-vertical lift.
From the Sweetser Collection; courtesy of Mr. and Mrs. William Warren

The houses of ill repute were permanently removed by the agent of the Prescott sisters, Charles Dale, who moved this old house, the Oracle House, to this site. Dale became governor during the 1950s. It is reported by one of his cronies that Dale once exclaimed, "If I kept all the company I am reported to have kept, I'd never have gotten any of my work done."
Courtesy of the Athenaeum

The Oracle House before it was moved from its second location in Haymarket Square to Water Street.
Courtesy of the Athenaeum

Another photo of the future Prescott Park and Strawbery Banke, Inc.
Courtesy of the Athenaeum

South Mill Bridge and vicinity in Portsmouth.
Courtesy of the Athenaeum

Modern photograph of the South Mill Pond in Portsmouth.
From the collection of Bruce E. Ingmire

The tollbooth from Portsmouth to Newcastle as it was in the early twentieth century. These bridges were first built in 1822 and united Portsmouth with Newcastle over Shapleigh's and Amazeen's islands. The bridge to Rye on the other end of Great Island was not built until 1874. Although the gazebo and flower gardens are no more, the old tollbooth, on the right, remains with its sunburst design still intact in 1989, although it is hidden by foliage.
Courtesy of the Athenaeum

A view of Pleasant Street taken in front of the post office and showing the precursor to 1989's Piscataqua Bank.
From the Sweetser Collection; courtesy of Mr. and Mrs. William Warren

A photograph of the old Jefferson Market taken in the 1870s. The Jefferson Market burned in the 1802 fire, but the walls remained standing, so the building was remodeled with first-floor stalls from which merchants could market their goods. The buildings on lower Pleasant Street were raised several floors after this picture was taken.
Courtesy of the Athenaeum

Market Square in a 1915 postcard view. In 1977 shade trees were once again introduced into the square.
From the collection of Bruce E. Ingmire

Market Street about 1870 showing those peculiar stanchions apparently used for anchoring awnings. Notice the gas lamps and cobblestones to the bottom left of the photo.
From the Sweetser Collection; courtesy of Mr. and Mrs. William Warren

161

Market Street about 1900 looking as it does today except for the evidence of traffic going in two directions.
From the collection of Bruce E. Ingmire

Hoyt and Dow on Market Street at the beginning of the century.
Courtesy of Morris Berry and family

In the 1600s this area was salt marsh surrounding the inlet and reaching into the area of today's Miller Avenue, where Lincoln Hill and Rumny Hill once marked the beginning of the upland. The millpond was connected by a brook (now the Langdon House driveway) to an inlet called Puddle Dock where the "common" at the museum at Strawbery Banke, Inc. is today. In those days high tide at the South Mill Pond also joined the North Mill Pond essentially where Middle and Bridge streets now exist. In the picture the wooden Universalist Church can be seen to the viewer's right. Just to the left of the stone Unitarian South Church is the old fire station with its tower for drying out fire hoses. Today that building is Baker-Wright.
Courtesy of the Athenaeum

J. P. Sweetser at 46 Market Street. The store featured household items from stoves to china in the pre-World War I era.
From the Sweetser Collection; courtesy of Mr. and Mrs. William Warren

A view of Pleasant Street about 1870 looking south away from Market Square. Pleasant Street was a gift to the city from John Pickering II to create a land route to his mill and the meetinghouse. This section of town was organized about 1670. Until that time the original land grants for Strawberry Bank were on Great Island, Sagamore Creek, and Cutts Cove to the north of Spring Hill. (The Dolphin Striker sits on Spring Hill in 1989.)

The wooden 1807 Universalist Church is prominent in the left of the photo and to its north is the "Old Parsonage," which was moved to Sturbridge Village in Massachusetts. This is where the Reverend Mr. Samuel Langdon lived and raised his family. Langdon was minister at the North Church and later served as president of Harvard during the American Revolution. The next house is the 1792 parsonage where Dr. Joseph Buckminister lived while he served at the North Church.

The Universalist Society was organized in Portsmouth in 1777. One of the early founders of the movement was Hosea Ballou who was descended from William Bellew of Dover. The first meetinghouse for the society was on Vaughan Street. This church was built in 1807 and was among the finest buildings in the town. It burned on March 28, 1896, and was replaced by the brick Universalist Church. For much of the nineteenth century this congregation was the largest in Portsmouth. The public way was being paved when the photo was being taken. From the Sweetser Collection; courtesy of Mr. and Mrs. William Warren

This view about 1890 includes the Italianate Call House that was removed to create the corner on today's Langdon Museum. Before that the Pennhallow House in Strawbery Banke, Inc. was situated on the site.
Courtesy of the Athenaeum

A view after the 1882 redesign of the Portsmouth Savings Bank, the Piscataqua Savings Bank, and the First National Bank building. The building was first erected as a bank after the 1802 fire destroyed the central district. In 1904 a further redesign took place, dividing the building and creating a Beaux Arts facade of granite on one side for the First National Bank and a Greek derived facade of limestone for the Portsmouth Savings Bank. The oldest bank building in the United States, it became the Shanley Real Estate Office in the 1970s. Shanley preserved the glass dome with the seal of New Hampshire that graces the main lobby.
Courtesy of the Athenaeum

This photo was taken about 1905 and is the site of the Indian Head Bank in 1989. The style of the center building, often called Victorian, is at this writing more properly called Renaissance. As one advocate of precise architectural information suggested, "Victorian" imparts about as much information as "white house." Note that the additions on the Exchange Block include the wide dormers that remain today. The brick sidewalk in the foreground is near the "bollards" that have been returned in today's restoration.
Courtesy of the Athenaeum

Market Square about 1915 showing the fountain that once quenched the thirst of horses transporting goods. About 1740, the time of the Great Awakening, a town pump served up spring water for residents Jothan Odiorne, John Rindge, and others who lived in homes that sur-rounded the then-residential square and its church.
From the collection of Bruce E. Ingmire

The Pythian Hall at the eastern entrance to Market Square about 1890. In 1989 the same building is the location of Alie's Jewelry Building. The late-nineteenth-century renovation reduced the floors from the original four floors to three. For a number of years Bernadette Alie graced Portsmouth with her smile, style, and grace. She passed away as this book was being written.
From the Sweetser Collection; courtesy of Mr. and Mrs. William Warren

The North Church showing the doors
open and either a peddler or traffic
officer under the umbrella. To the right
of the church the next building is
Hunking Wentworth's 1730 home,
showing more of its original form than
is obvious today with its 1950s aluminum facade. Further to the right is the
classical decoration on the theater which
is said to still be intact under the present-
day marquee. Further right is the Rogers
Building, which was razed and replaced
with a modern storefront. It burned in
the 1960s, leaving one of those gaps in
the streetscapes of Portsmouth that
quickly became a parking lot.
From the Sweetser Collection; courtesy of
Mr. and Mrs. William Warren

Trolleys in the Square and evidence of
the perilous hike one once had to take to
cross the Square in the days of early
automobiles. The success of Green's
Drug store may have resulted from aspir-
in sold to weary citizens who had just
dodged the traffic in crossing the Square
and were overcome with horror at the
thought of retracing their steps. This
theory is substantiated by the fact that
the drugstore disappeared a few years
after the improvements created a more
manageable crossing of Market Square.
From the collection of Bruce E. Ingmire

Further proof of the driving madness in
the Square is this picture reminding the
readers that for many years there was
two-way traffic.
From the collection of Bruce E. Ingmire

The Peduzzi Building, owned by an Italian immigrant, was demolished in 1890. The Romany billboard is a reminder of the larger 1970s billboard mural that was in Market Square to cover the collapse of the Pierce Building in which Foster's is located presently. In the 1880s the top floor with the skylight was the location of a photographer named Newell. Peduzzi was a Roman Catholic and he often allowed Dover's parish priest to come to this house and say mass for Portsmouth's Catholics. In 1989 Harvey's Bakery is located on the site. Courtesy of the Athenaeum

The corner of Bow and Market streets
in Portsmouth about 1880 with cobblestones for the street pavement.
Courtesy of Strawbery Banke, Inc.

A view of Lower Congress before urban
renewal projects and highway proposals
created a roadway through the old North
End. Urban renewal in Portsmouth had
no genius like Hausmann in Paris.
When Hausmann created the wide
boulevards in Paris, he repalced the old
buildings with new ones and kept the
neighborhoods. Portsmouth's North End
was devasted but the neighborhood was
not replaced, and that section never recovered. It was the result of this short-
sighted condemn-and-destroy policy that
caused certain foresighted citizens to
begin programs to preserve and restore
sections of Portsmouth for posterity. The
house on the right is the eighteenth-
century Treadwell mansion, which stood
opposite the library. At one time Dr.
Cutter, Gov. John Wentworth's personal
physician who turned to the patriot
cause, occupied the mansion. Later
Charles Dale had offices in the mansion.
From the collection of Bruce E. Ingmire

Odd Fellows Hall at Fleet and Congress
about 1920. The site is that of the
former City Hall. In the back can be
seen the one-story garage that replaced
the stone stable.
Courtesy of Strawbery Banke, Inc.

9
THE CHALLENGE OF THE PRESENT

Today, seacoast New Hampshire is one of the most rapidly growing areas in the entire country. Capitalizing on the proximity of Boston and the explosion of business related to modern technology, the faces of the old towns of the Piscataqua are almost daily altered. The lack of a state income tax and sales tax provides an attraction to corporations that wish to locate here. New enterprises proliferate, bringing with them more people, necessitating the expansion of services and facilities. Megalopolis creeps northward; shopping malls, housing developments, motels, and restaurants are scattered across the landscape as though flung outward from the hub by centrifugal force.

These important changes have forced a restructuring of the economic base of the area. Just as fishing, the mast trade, shipbuilding, and agriculture gave way to manufacturing textiles, shoes, and ale, so today the average worker is likely to be employed in a job that is service-related or is involved in advanced technology, or to use a more familiar phrase, "high technology."

Apple picking. During World War II, the Piscataqua suffered a labor shortage, so volunteers pitched in to help with the apple harvest. This picture was taken at the orchard of Leon Watson in Durham in 1943. University of New Hampshire Dean Everett Sackett is on the ladder. Sackett served the university as dean of students and later as dean of the College of Liberal Arts.
Courtesy of Dorothy Watson

Exeter provides a useful example of the type of transition that has occurred throughout the seacoast region. At the close of World War II the Exeter Manufacturing Company employed 530 men and women and turned out twelve million yards of gray goods (unfinished) and fifty million yards of finished goods annually. In 1955 all cotton goods were discontinued and replaced by synthetics. In 1966, in accordance with an all-too-familiar trend, Milliken Industries, Inc., based in South Carolina, purchased the one-hundred-and-forty-year-old company. The Exeter division of Milliken was known as Clemson Fabrics, but before long, weaving was discontinued and industrial finishing was substituted. By 1980 increased foreign imports priced lower than locally produced goods forced the plant to close.

Shoe companies in Newmarket, such as Little Yankee Shoe, found it difficult to continue, and now Timberland Footwear maintains a factory outlet only to market shoes.

Ironically, in Exeter, Newmarket, and Dover, the mammoth brick edifices where once workers toiled manufacturing shoes and textiles, today have been converted into condominiums providing dwelling places for the more affluent descendants of those workers. The need for housing has created a plethora of all manner of facilities: condominiums, apartments, cluster housing, and trailer parks as well as the traditional detached homes. Green

fields and arable land, once dotted with grazing animals and waving grain now bear the imprint of development to accommodate a rising population. Seedy and shabby town neighborhoods have been revitalized by artistic elements in the arriving migration of young professionals. Soon, exposed brick, bare oak, large windows, and indoor plants mark the process now identified as gentrification. Neighborhoods once marked for urban renewal are now described as "upscale."

The improvements are not confined to housing. In central districts or "downtowns," as New Englanders call them, brick facades covered with plastic tiles, aluminum siding, and marked by garish neon lights were uncovered. Enlightened restoration stripped away anachronistic accretions and produced aesthetic impressions of past halcyonic eras. In Dover, Portsmouth and Durham, fountains, period lighting, trees, and landscaping have produced views of uncluttered buildings and enhanced the squares and thoroughfares. Buildings of exceptional beauty like the Portsmouth Athenaeum and the Ammi Burnham Young Post Office of the 1850s have been restored to their pristine state. Creativity is evident in Dover; instead of demolishing the old Methodist church, the sturdy late-nineteenth-century Gothic edifice has been renovated and reincarnated as a residence for senior citizens. The Farragut School in Portsmouth has also been converted to

housing for senior citizens. Where they once memorized their three R's, golden-agers now consume croissants.

Frank Jones's old malt house in Portsmouth survives as a multi-purpose building with restaurants, a health club with a swimming pool, a tanning parlor, and a beauty salon. Citizens of the seacoast reflect an attitude of appreciation about facades and appearances that are to be found elsewhere throughout the country. In the New Hampshire seacoast, however, because of its age, the architectural variety spans some three hundred years, providing a texture and reflecting a variety that is unmatched in most other parts of the nation.

That urge to protect and preserve the buildings has developed throughout most of this century and reflects a maturing of American aesthetics. The Colonial Dames of New Hampshire and the Society for the Preservation of New England Antiquities, among other groups, have assumed responsibility for maintaining important homes such as the Moffat-Ladd House and the Richard Jackson House in Portsmouth. The state of New Hampshire has acquired the Governor Benning Wentworth Home on Little Harbor from the Coolidge family, that wished to see it preserved in a pristine form for future generations to study the idiosyncracies of the style. Other private and local groups maintain the Warner House and the Went-worth-Gardiner House in Portsmouth. Historic churches

173

This Free French sailor was the guest of Mr. and Mrs. Louis DeRochemont at a clambake in Newington in 1941. A number of Free French visited during World War II.

like the Episcopalian St. John's, the successor to the Colonial Queen's Chapel, and the Unitarian Universalist church, the historic South Church, are now on the Register of Historic Buildings, as is the entire central district of Portsmouth.

Strawberry Banke, Inc., a museum complex of primarily timber framed buildings of at least two centuries in age, some of which have been furnished in the period of their erection, has been a leader in authentic restoration in the area. Drawing preservationists and artists to the seacoast for the last thirty years with craft shops and educational exhibits, Strawberry Banke, Inc. has demonstrated what citizens with foresight accomplish in the face of the threat of federal urban renewal projects which advocate the demolition of entire quaint sections of similar towns throughout the northeast. A Portsmouth librarian, Dorothy Vaughan, who was not a native but nonetheless knew the historic importance of the area is credited with first sounding the alarm that a battle to preserve these sites was imminent. The museum has become a symbol of the spirit of preservation and a leading attraction for the town.

The threat of rapid growth was stayed by the awareness that a vital and unique part of the region's heritage might be lost forever. In the 1980s, the move to save man's record of achievement has been joined by those who wish to save some of the open fields and seacoast wetlands and to end pollution which threatens the lifeblood of the area. Once people had realized that the buildings constituted a significant collection reflecting the social, political, and economic history of the seacoast, the movement to save land in its natural state followed. These movements have

helped to underline a sentimental attachment to the seacoast which is both romantic and ephemeral.

Historic district commissions and land trusts have been instituted to further the causes. The rise of these movements has created a conflict with those who see development as necessary for the growth that makes jobs and economic well-being. The outcome will hopefully be a moderate approach that preserves the past and promotes the economic health of the seacoast. Some approaches are the Portsmouth community's Market Square Day Weekend and Somersworth's International Children's Festival.

These attempts to offset the proliferation of malls and reinvigorate the downtowns have been well received.

The seacoast has witnessed significant physical changes in recent years. The construction of Pease Air Force Base in Newington ranks high on this list. Built in the 1950s as a Strategic Air Command Base for the deployment of B-52 bombers in the event of nuclear war, it has augmented the Naval Shipyard's contribution to the economic base of the region. Today it is an important base for KC-135s, the mid-air refueling ships.

In the mid-1970s business interests of Aristotle Onassis proposed an oil refinery in Durham, which sparked a local protest against a proposed pipeline to Rye and off-shore loading facilities at the Isles of Shoals. Widespread opposition to the project caused its defeat. The movement called Save Our Shores was developed by Nancy Sandberg and supported by people like Representative Dudley Dudley, and Phyllis Bennett, owner and publisher of *Publick Occurrences*, helped to defeat the program. The event awakened interests in the marshlands,

wetlands, and conservation in general that has seen the
rise of such conservation-minded groups as the Friends of
Odiorne Point and helped to spur the development of
water treatment facilities on Great Bay and the associated
river tributaries. In the end the efforts of Onassis floun-
dered on the shoals of "home rule." This time development came up against a New England tradition of local
autonomy associated with the traditional town meeting.
While the Onassis refinery suffered defeat, the support for
the Seabrook Nuclear Power Plant is so evenly divided in
the community that it has struggled through attempts to
derail its implementation.

The Seabrook Nuclear Power Plant is an issue as yet
unresolved. Although now completed, the first reactor has
not as yet provided power to the region, for it has been
plagued by financial problems and difficulties in obtain-
ing approval for its plans for evacuation of local residents
and visitors in the event of an emergency. The vocal opposition of anti-nuclear groups has been one of the clearest
examples of local involvement in the decision making
process. Local groups employing the town meeting system have become a standard of anti-nuclear opposition
throughout the United States. Seabrook has become as
synonymous with the protest of average citizens against
nuclear power as Almogordo has come to represent
nuclear development.

The historic institution of local control is in jeopardy
today. In a society increasingly complex, it is difficult for
selectmen as part-time administrators to deal with projects
involving an increasing number of state and federal reg-
ulations. Funding for many projects depends upon help
from agencies far removed from the locality. Symptomatic

This barn was the first building completed on the new campus. The class of 1892 graduated there and it burned *in 1894.*
Courtesy of the University of New Hampshire Media Services

of these changes is the new town charter adopted by Durham in 1987. After 250 years of traditional New England town government, the new charter mandates a town council and a town manager. The old order gives way to the prevailing bureaucratic structure.

Culturally, the seacoast is distinguished among areas north of Boston. The University of New Hampshire, founded in 1866, offers a variety of programs and degrees from the bachelor to the doctorate. Concerts and dramatic productions are offered at the Johnson theater. Visitors are drawn to the athletic events as well as exhibits at the Paul Creative Arts Center. Phillips Exeter Academy, one of the nation's most distinguished preparatory schools, offers many cultural opportunities to the residents of the seacoast as well. Its new library, designed by Louis Kahn, is an addition to the architectural heritage of the region. Portsmouth's A Theater-by-the-Sea closed its doors recently after an outstanding quarter of a century of innovative theater. However, new theater companies still flourish in the seacoast, including Durham's Mill Pond Center, Portsmouth's Generic Theater, PAPA, Pontine Movement Theater, Dover's Garrison Players, and Exeter Theater Players.

Journalism has flourished in New Hampshire since 1756, when Daniel Fowle first published his *New Hampshire Gazette.* In 1765 Portsmouth was one of only five cities in colonial America to have more than one newspaper published each week. The *Gazette* and the *Portsmouth Mercury,* published by Thomas Furber, became embroiled in the controversy between patriot and Loyalist previous to the American Revolution. While Daniel Fowle walked a tightrope of moderation, his own nephew who published in Exeter was eventually proscribed as a Tory.

Over the years newspaper writers and publishers have contributed to the recording of local history. Charles Brewster's *Rambles* remains a classic of the early Portsmouth history concentrating on the era of the Revolution and post-revolutionary period. Ray Brighton, former editor of the *Portsmouth Herald,* managed to retire and devote himself totally to local history after the publication of a commemorative history in which he argued that settlers "came to fish," quoting from Cotton Mather's *Magnalia Christi Americana.* Dr. Charles Clark, professor of History at the University of New Hampshire, started his distinguished career as a writer for the Providence, Rhode Island, *Journal and Evening Bulletin.* His *The Eastern Frontier: The Settlement of Northern New England* has become a standard for anyone launching into early history of the region. Other historians have been encouraged by publisher Peter Randall and his patron Joseph Sawtelle both of whom have encouraged local writers like Richard Winslow to investigate the maritime history of the region. Other writers with local and regional influence include Charles Simic, poet, May Sarton, poet, John Irving, novelist and a former Exeter resident and UNH graduate, and Richard Candee, architectural historian. Olive Tardiff, Anne Malloy, and Esther Buffler have contributed to children's fiction.

Newspapers continue to be an important source of information in the seacoast. Portsmouth alone has three important journals including the *Herald, Portsmouth Magazine,* and the *Portsmouth Press.* The last is owned by Ottaway, a division of Dow-Jones, the publishers of the *Wall Street Journal,* who have invested heavily in a number of local papers under the umbrella of the Rockingham County Newspapers. Dover's *Foster's Daily Democrat* and Exeter's *Exeter News-Letter* boast long and

Thompson Hall at the University of New Hampshire was named for Benjamin Thompson, an early benefactor of the school. The building is shown here under construction in 1892-1893. Classes were held in this building when the campus became operational in 1893. The building held the administration offices, as it does today, as well as a library, a museum, and an assembly hall.

Originally named New Hampshire College of Agriculture and Mechanic Arts, the school was first chartered in 1866 under the Morrill Land Grant College Act and was housed at Dartmouth College until 1893, when it moved to Durham after the bequest by Thompson. The institution was re-chartered in 1923 as the University of New Hampshire.
Courtesy of the University of New Hampshire Media Services

distinguished careers in bringing the news to local residents. The seacoast once again has become a haunt and home to a number of writers who contribute to these papers. Writers for the national press like Kathy Gunst and Peter Lemos have been drawn to the area because of its literary traditions.

The New Hampshire seacoast remains after 350 years a vital place. In many ways, in both its problems and its accomplishments, it is a microcosm of the entire country. The dialogue among conservationists, preservationists and developers, the increasing intrusion of state and federal government in local affairs, the severe adjustments imposed upon the economy and the efforts to accommodate a rapidly increasing population, all require titanic efforts in the search for creative solutions.

What would those early pioneers think if they could stroll the streets of the old towns today? How would they react to the bridges spanning the entrance to the Piscataqua? Imagine the shock of seeing the mammoth ships that now course their way up the river. Think of the wonderment that would fill the face of Edward Hilton standing on the shores of today's Great Bay as huge jets from Pease Air Force base thunder into the "wild blue yonder." Few of the Puritans that first settled the shores of Dover Point could imagine allowing their sons and daughters an afternoon of leisure—skimming the calm waters of Back River on multi-colored wind-surfing craft like dragonflies in search of sustenance. The old order has changed indeed.

Doris Bean, a native of Newington and a graduate of Smith College, served as the recorder (registrar) of the University of New Hampshire for many years. She was a friend to many generations of students in an age when records were kept in stout ledgers.
Courtesy of the Langdon Library, Newington, New Hampshire

177

*Aerial view of the University
of New Hampshire.
Courtesy of the University of
New Hampshire Media Services*

*Thomas Williams of Durham, New
Hampshire, is the recipient of numerous
literary prizes including the National
Book Award. Born in Duluth, Minnesota,
he has taught in the University of New
Hampshire's English Department since
1958. A graduate of the university, he is
the author of many critically acclaimed
novels and short stories.
Courtesy of the University of
New Hampshire Media Services*

*This view shows the old Exeter Manu-
facturing Company from across the
Exeter River as it appeared in 1988,
when condominium conversion was
under way.*
Photo by Paul Farrell

*The tugs near Ceres Street, Portsmouth,
in 1988.*
Photo by Paul Farrell

Portsmouth's Market Square with the brick Romanesque-style building that houses Harvey's Bakery of Dover and several apartments. This building replaced the Peduzzi Building.
From the collection of Bruce E. Ingmire

Today Market Square has become home to Portsmouth's annual opening of the summer season, Market Square Day, which is held on a weekend in June traditionally picked by a committee called the Board of Directors of Pro Portsmouth. This group spends most of the winter consulting soothsayers, Indian medicine men, tarot card readers, astrologers, and various other predictors of the future in the hopes of controlling the weather. The photo shows the start of the road race that has become a premier event for runners.
Courtesy of Pro Portsmouth

The Athenaeum in 1977 with celebrators at the first Market Square Day. Notice that the raking cornice is missing on right of the Athenaeum. It was replaced when Foster's restored the Pierce building after it collapsed during renovations about 1983.
From the collection of Bruce E. Ingmire

183

View of Adams Point in Durham, where the home of "Reformation John" Adams once stood. He was an itinerant preacher in the nineteenth century and a member of a collateral branch of the family of President John Adams. The home was demolished in the 1970s. Today it is the site of the University of New Hampshire Estuarine Laboratory, the Jackson Lab. Courtesy of the University of New Hampshire Media Services

Jackson house, built in 1664, is the oldest house in New Hampshire. After the earliest housing, this style predominated in New England. It is now owned by the Society for the Preservation of New England Antiquities and shown by appointment only. Richard Jackson was a cooper who worked for the Cutts family and the Hulls, who were related through marriage to the Starr and Fernside families. These families made up the early Puritan oligarchy of Portsmouth. Since many families like the Walfords, Sherburnes, Wentworths, Waltons, and others of the period living on Great Island had all been dismissed from the Boston area for various reasons, Bostonians came to mockingly refer to the area where the Puritan oligarchy settled as "Christian Shores." Like the term "Puritan" itself, what had been used mockingly came to be used by residents with pride.
From the collection of Bruce E. Ingmire

This house on Gates Street, Portsmouth, is the birthplace of James T. Fields, once the editor and publisher of Atlantic Monthly, *and represents the transition from the asymmetrical early wooden architecture to the balanced, appointed style of the Georgian era when facade was so important.*
Photo by Paul Farrell

Moffat Ladd House was built by a wealthy merchant. This house was later occupied by William Whipple, signer of the Declaration of Independence. According to tradition, the Chestnut tree near the house was planted by Whipple in 1776. The house is now owned by the Colonial Dames of New Hampshire and is also a fine example of Georgian architecture.
Photo by Paul Farrell

Patch House on Court Street, Portsmouth, represents a private home built in the Greek Revival style, which is noted for placing the gable end of the houses to the street in the mode of a Greek temple. Photo by Bruce E. Ingmire

Portsmouth Athenaeum, a private library dedicated to Portsmouth and New Hampshire history, was an important contributor to this work. The Federal style of this brick building developed after the American Revolution to create a formal architecture expressing the spirit of the new republic. It is at one time light, refined, and classical. Photo by Bruce E. Ingmire

The Bottle Baptist Church, Hampton Falls, is reported to have been the recipient of one of Frank Jones's philanthropic gifts. It is believed that the crown of the steeple is either in the shape of or actually contains a bottle.
Photo by Paul Farrell

Frank Jones Brewery on Islington Street in Portsmouth.
Photo by Paul Farrell

St. John's Episcopal Church, also in the Federal style.
Photo by Paul Farrell

Portsmouth harbor.
Photo by Paul Farrell

Memorial Bridge at its fully opened position to accommodate a tall ship during the 1980s. America has recently engaged in a love affair with tall ships, initiated at the bicentennial of the Declaration of Independence. Visits of these inspiring ships to Portsmouth have recalled the great days of the sailing vessel.
Photo by Bruce E. Ingmire

The sailors and cadets aboard one of the tall ships, the Simon Bolivar *from Colombia which visited Portsmouth in June of 1988. One of the shrines that they visited was the house in which John Paul, who took the surname Jones, lived for nine months while overseeing the construction of the* Ranger.
From the collection of Bruce E. Ingmire; photo by Suzanne Benn

Recreational sailing at the mouth of the
Piscataqua. Photo taken about 1980.
Photo by Bruce E. Ingmire

Market Square Day, 1988. An eleven year old event, started to re-focus attention on the commercial center of Portsmouth, Market Square Day was the largest event of its nature in New Hampshire in 1988.
Photo by Bruce E. Ingmire

The Market Square Day Road Race, 1988.
Photo by Bruce E. Ingmire

Contemporary photo of the harbor at Ceres Street, Portsmouth, and the departure of a container ship which can carry a cargo equal to a fleet of eighteenth-century vessels.
Photo by Bruce E. Ingmire

Harbor at Ceres Street, Portsmouth.
Photo by Bruce E. Ingmire

Another ship departs the Ceres Street harbor.
Photo by Bruce E. Ingmire

*The North Church steeple decked out for
Market Square Day.
Photo by Bruce E. Ingmire*

Cabot Street building being transformed into condominiums, the trend in recent days.
Photo by Paul Farrell

The remodeled coal burning electricity plant and now office condominiums, continuing the trend called gentrification. Photo by Paul Farrell

The Atlantic Ocean.
Photo by Paul Farrell

Sunset over the Piscataqua.
Photo by Paul Farrell

BIBLIOGRAPHY

The entrance to the Piscataqua River at Newcastle, New Hampshire.
Photo by Paul Farrell

Adams, Charles Francis. *Three Episodes in Massachusetts History.* New York: Russell and Russell, 1965 (1892).

Bell, Charles. *History of Exeter, New Hampshire.* Boston, Massachusetts: J. E. Farwell and Company, 1888.

Brewster, C. W. *Brewster's Rambles About Portsmouth, Facsimile of the 1873 Edition,* Somersworth, New Hampshire, 1871.

Brighton, Ray. *Frank Jones: King of the Alemakers.* Portsmouth, New Hampshire: Peter Randall, 1976.

——————. *Port of Portsmouth: Ships and the Cotton Trade 1783-1829.* Portsmouth, New Hampshire: Peter E. Randall, 1986.

——————. *The Prescott Story.* Portsmouth, New Hampshire: The Portsmouth Maritime Society, 1982.

——————. *They Came to Fish.* Portsmouth, New Hampshire: The Portsmouth 350 Inc., 1973.

Daniell, Jere R. *Colonial New Hampshire: A History.* Millwood, New York: KTO Press, 1981.

Getchell, Sylvia. *The Tide Turns on the Lamprey-Vignettes in the Life of a River: A History of Newmarket, New Hampshire.* Newmarket, New Hampshire: S. P. Getchell, 1984.

Gilmore, Robert C. *New Hampshire Literature.* Hanover, New Hampshire: The University Press of New England, 1981.

Morison, Esther Forbes and Morison, Elting E. *New Hampshire - A Bicentennial History.* New York: W. W. Norton, Inc., 1976.

Saltonstall, William. *Ports of the Piscataqua.* Cambridge, Massachusetts: Harvard University Press, 1941.

Tardiff, Olive. *The Exeter-Squamscott, River of Many Uses.* Rye, New Hampshire: C. R. C., 1986.

Thompson, Mary R. *Landmarkes of Ancient Dover, Durham, New Hampshire.* Durham, New Hampshire: Durham Historical Society, 1965.

Wadleigh, George. *Notable Events in the History of Dover, New Hampshire.* Boston, Massachusetts: Tufts College, 1913.

Whitehouse, Robert A. *Port of Dover.* Portsmouth, New Hampshire: Portsmouth Marine Society, 1988.

Winslow, Richard E. *Portsmouth Built Submarines of the Portsmouth Naval Shipyard.* Portsmouth, New Hampshire: Portsmouth Marine Society, 1988.

——————. *The Piscataqua Gundalow.* Portsmouth, New Hampshire: Portsmouth Marine Society, 1983.

Vanderventer, David E. *The Emergence of Provincial New Hampshire.* Baltimore, Maryland: Johns Hopkins University Press, 1976.

ABOUT THE AUTHORS

Bruce E. Ingmire was born in Saratoga Springs, New York, educated in New York state, and graduated from the University of Rochester in Rochester, New York. In 1970, he joined VISTA and was assigned to Concord, New Hampshire. He has remained in New Hampshire since that assignment. Employed by TWA for a number of years as a flight attendant, he commuted to New York and Boston for work. In his free time he spent hours acquainting himself with the colonial history of the state. In 1986, he was accepted in a master's program in history at the University of New Hampshire in Durham where he will be completing his studies at the end of 1988. A resident of Portsmouth, New Hampshire, for over a decade, Ingmire has given walking tours and become identified with that segment of the community involved in history and restoration. With this background he was a logical choice for Dr. Gilmore to invite to assist him in the authorship of *The New Hampshire Seacoast.*

Robert C. Gilmore, a native Vermonter, graduated from the University of Vermont, McGill, and Yale University. While at Yale, he was a Nathan Hale Fellow. He is a professor of history at the University of New Hampshire where he has served as director of the College of Liberal Arts Honors Program and director of the Ford Foundation M.A.-3 Program. He teaches courses in early American history at the university. His book *New Hampshire Literature* appeared in 1981. He is also the author of articles on Northern New England history and is currently engaged in research on allegories and the American Revolution.